# LONDuN

## TRAVEL GUIDE 2025

Explore the Best Places to Visit, Local Culture, History, Traditions, Tourist Attractions, and Culinary Experiences With Budget-Friendly Itinerary and Insider Tips

JOHN S. MARLER

**COPYRIGHT © JOHN S. MARLER 2024**

All rights reserved. No part of this publication may be reproduced, distributed, or transmitted in any form or by any means, including photocopying, recording, or other electronic or mechanical methods, without the prior written permission of the publisher, except in the case of brief quotations embodied in critical reviews and certain other non-commercial uses permitted by copyright law.

# TABLE OF CONTENTS

**INTRODUCTION** .................................................................. 7

    What's New for 2025? .................................................. 8

    Top Reasons to Visit London This Year ................... 12

**CHAPTER 1** ........................................................................ 18

**Getting Around London** ................................................. 18

    Navigating London's Transportation System ........... 21

    Biking, Walking, and Eco-Friendly Options ............ 27

    Tips for Efficient and Stress-Free Travel .................. 29

**CHAPTER 2** ........................................................................ 32

**Where to Stay in London** .............................................. 32

    Accommodation Options for Every Budget ............. 35

    Best Neighborhoods to Stay Based on Interests ....... 38

    Accessibility-Friendly Lodging Choices .................. 41

**CHAPTER 3** ........................................................................ 47

**Top Attractions and Must-Sees** ................................... 47

    Iconic Landmarks and When to Visit ....................... 51

    World-Class Museums and Galleries ........................ 54

    Unique London Tours for an Insider's View ............ 58

**CHAPTER 4** ........................................................................ 65

**Off-the-Beaten-Path London** ............................................................ 65

    Hidden Neighborhoods with Local Appeal ............... 71

    Quirky Attractions You Won't Find on the Usual Lists ................................................................................................ 78

    Local Favorites: Pubs, Cafes, and Secret Gardens ... 84

**CHAPTER 5** .................................................................................. 90

**Suggested Itineraries** ................................................................ 90

    1, 3, and 5-Day Itineraries for All Interests ............... 96

    Seasonal Activities and Events to Plan Around....... 103

    Themed Itineraries: Royal, Historical, Family- ....... 107

    Friendly ................................................................................ 107

    Budget-Friendly Itinerary Planner ............................ 111

**CHAPTER 6** ................................................................................ 117

**Dining and Nightlife**................................................................ 117

    Classic British Dishes and Where to Find Them .... 122

    Top Food Markets for Every Taste......................... 127

    Neighborhood-Specific Restaurant Recommendations ................................................................................................ 134

**CHAPTER 7** ................................................................................ 141

**Shopping and Souvenirs**........................................................... 141

    Famous Shopping Districts and What to Expect .... 146

Boutiques and Markets for Unique Finds ............... 151

Souvenir Guide: Take Home a Piece of London .... 157

## CHAPTER 8 ................................................................ 163

## Seasonal Events and Festivals ................................... 163

Annual Events ........................................................ 166

What's Happening in 2025? Special Citywide Events
................................................................................ 169

Monthly Event Highlights ..................................... 173

## CHAPTER 9 ................................................................ 177

## Practical Tips and Travel Essentials ........................ 177

Budget-Friendly Tips for Exploring London .......... 180

Cultural Etiquette: How to Blend In Like a Local .. 183

Safety, Emergency Contacts, and Health Tips ........ 186

Packing Guide for Every Season ............................ 193

## CHAPTER 10 .............................................................. 197

## Day Trips and Excursions ......................................... 197

Top Day Trips from London ................................... 202

How to Get to Windsor, Bath, the Cotswolds, and More
................................................................................ 207

Themed Day Trips: Castles, Countryside, and Historic Towns ..................................................................... 212

**CHAPTER 11** .................................................................. **215**

**Sustainable Travel in London**................................. **215**

    Green Hotels, Restaurants, and Activities ............ 218

    Eco-Friendly Itineraries and Transportation Options ................................................................................. 222

    Reducing Your Environmental Footprint .............. 224

**CHAPTER 12** .................................................................. **228**

**Planning Tools and Resources** ................................ **228**

    High-Resolution City and Neighborhood Maps ..... 231

    Essential Apps and Websites for Easy Navigation . 233

    Local Language Tips and Common British Phrases 236

**CHAPTER 13** .................................................................. **240**

**Insider Tips and FAQs** ............................................... **240**

    FAQs: What Every Visitor Wants to Know .......... 245

    Insider Secrets for Avoiding Crowds and Finding Hidden Gems ....................................................... 252

    "London Like a Local": Tips to Experience the City Authentically........................................................ 259

**CONCLUSION** ............................................................... **267**

# INTRODUCTION

Welcome to London Travel Guide 2025, your important resource for experiencing one of the world's most captivating cities. Whether you are visiting for the first time or returning to discover new layers of this iconic city, this guide is designed to provide you with practical advice, insider insights, and up-to-date information to make the most of your trip.

London, a city known for its rich past, diverse culture, and boundless energy, has something for every traveler. From the grandeur of its historical landmarks to the buzz of its modern streets, London continues to evolve while keeping the unique characteristics that have made it one of the most visited cities in the world.

In 2025, London's dynamic scene is filled with exciting chances to explore. This guide will help you find must-see attractions, hidden gems, and the best spots to relax, dine, and shop. You'll find detailed itineraries that fit different interests and timelines, tips for exploring sustainably, and advice for experiencing the city like a local.

London is more than just a destination—it's a call to experience culture, creativity, history, and the unexpected. This guide is your key to unlocking everything the city has to offer. It's time to explore London in a way that suits you—whether you're drawn to its art, history, or vibrant neighborhoods, the city's endless options are waiting for you. Let's begin your journey through London in 2025.

## What's New for 2025?

London in 2025 is brimming with fresh experiences, developments, and attractions, ensuring that even returning visitors have something new to discover. The city continues to change, offering an exciting blend of modern innovation and classic charm. Here's a glimpse at what's ready for you in London this year:

1. The London Eye's New VR Experience The iconic London Eye has launched a thrilling virtual reality experience that adds an extra layer of excitement to your ride. Take your view of the city to the next level with immersive 360-degree visuals that transport you through

London's sites like never before. It's a perfect way to see the city from a whole new viewpoint.

2. The West End's Revamped Theater District
2025 marks the relaunch of several famous theaters in London's West End. With cutting-edge technologies, revamped interiors, and an even more diverse range of performances, this area is now more accessible and exciting than ever. Expect more interactive shows, diverse casts, and a new wave of theater experiences that appeal to all tastes.

3. Greenwich Park's New Eco-Conscious Visitor Centre
As part of a larger effort to make London more sustainable, Greenwich Park has revealed a new eco-conscious visitor center, featuring interactive exhibits on the park's history, wildlife, and sustainable practices. It's the perfect place to start a visit to one of London's most cherished Royal Parks, giving insights into both its natural beauty and its role in the city's green future.

4. The Opening of the National Art Gallery Expansion
The National Gallery is set to open a major expansion in 2025, giving even more space for world-renowned art

collections and temporary exhibits. The new wing promises to bring together classic masterpieces and modern works in a more accessible and engaging layout, making it a must-see for art lovers of all kinds.

5. The King's Cross Redevelopment
The King's Cross area, already a hub of regeneration, is unveiling new cultural spaces, galleries, and entertainment places this year. The newly completed Coal Drops Yard, a stylish shopping and dining area, now features even more high-end boutiques, cafes, and a new art gallery. This is a prime location for a day of shopping, eating, and discovering the modern face of London.

6. London's New Floating Cinema
For something truly special, London's Thames is now home to a floating cinema. This innovative outdoor cinema experience allows tourists to watch classic films and new releases while seated in boats that float along the river. It's the ultimate way to enjoy a night out in the city under the stars with beautiful riverside views.

7. Expanded Bike and Scooter Share Programs
With London's commitment to sustainability, 2025 sees a

big expansion of its bike and scooter-sharing programs. The city's improved cycling lanes and eco-friendly transportation choices make it easier than ever to explore London on two wheels, whether you're going to iconic landmarks or hidden gems off the beaten path.

8. New International Dining Experiences
London's dining scene has always been one of the world's most exciting, and 2025 brings even more innovative places to the city. From immersive dining experiences inspired by popular films and television to pop-up food markets serving global street food, there are endless chances to taste flavors from around the world. Be sure to explore the latest openings for a true dining adventure.

9. The Sky Garden's New Rooftop Bar
The Sky Garden has always been a favorite for panoramic views of London, but in 2025, it has improved the experience with a new rooftop bar. Offering stunning vistas of the city's skyline and a range of creative drinks, it's the ideal spot for a stylish evening out, enjoying the view as the city lights twinkle below.

10. 2025 Festivals and Special Events
London's calendar is packed with exciting new events in 2025, including an expanded line-up for the Summer Music Festival in Hyde Park, the debut of the London Global Film Festival, and the return of long-awaited street festivals celebrating the city's various cultures. These one-of-a-kind events will offer unique ways to immerse yourself in London's lively arts scene.

## Top Reasons to Visit London This Year

London in 2025 is an exhilarating blend of timeless traditions and exciting new innovations, making it the ideal location for first-time travelers and seasoned explorers alike. Whether you're captivated by its rich past, thriving cultural scene, or forward-thinking urban developments, there are plenty of compelling reasons to experience London this year. Here's why 2025 is the perfect time to visit:

1. A Thriving Arts and Culture Scene
London's image as a global cultural hub has never been more exciting. With the expansion of iconic institutions

like the National Gallery, the British Museum, and the Tate Modern, 2025 offers even more immersive and interactive exhibits. New gallery spaces and world-class art collections are making it a must-visit for art lovers, while the revamped West End is bringing fresh and diverse theater productions to the stage, elevating the city's cultural environment.

2. Groundbreaking New Attractions
2025 introduces cutting-edge attractions like the London Eye's new Virtual Reality experience and the floating cinema on the Thames, giving unique ways to experience the city. Whether you're soaring high above the city's skyline or watching a classic film on the water, London is constantly reinventing itself to offer tourists thrilling new experiences.

3. Sustainability and Green Initiatives
London is leading the way with its dedication to sustainability. In 2025, visitors will find more eco-friendly hotels, restaurants, and events than ever before. From expanded bike-sharing programs and electric buses to green spaces like the redesigned Greenwich Park Visitor Centre, London is becoming increasingly

environmentally conscious, allowing you to enjoy the city while adding to its greener future.

4. Festivals and Special Events

London's calendar of fairs in 2025 is packed with new and exciting events. Whether it's the Summer Music Festival in Hyde Park, the London Global Film Festival, or different cultural celebrations that showcase the city's diversity, there's always something happening. These events offer unforgettable ways to connect with London's rich heritage and vibrant global community, creating moments that will stay with you long after you leave.

5. Unforgettable Dining Experiences

London's culinary scene continues to change, with a mix of Michelin-starred restaurants, global street food, and innovative dining experiences. In 2025, London's gastronomic offerings will include everything from immersive dining inspired by films to the latest foreign food markets. Whether you're enjoying a traditional Sunday roast or sampling cutting-edge dishes, London's food scene is sure to surprise and delight.

6. World-Class Shopping
Whether you're browsing luxury boutiques on Bond Street or exploring trendy markets like Borough Market and Camden Lock, London's shopping areas are filled with endless possibilities. 2025 also sees the launch of new concept stores and pop-up shops that redefine the shopping experience, offering everything from sustainable clothes to quirky British designs. London is a shopper's paradise, with something for every taste and price.

7. London's Green Spaces
Escape the hustle and bustle by visiting London's incredible parks and gardens. From the iconic Hyde Park and Regent's Park to the lesser-known gems like Hampstead Heath and the Kyoto Garden in Holland Park, the city offers countless chances to unwind. These lush green spaces are great for picnics, leisurely walks, and soaking in London's tranquil side amidst the urban energy.

8. The Royal Experience
The Royal Family's presence continues to shape the essence of London, and 2025 offers unique chances to

delve deeper into Britain's royal heritage. Tour Buckingham Palace, visit Kensington Palace, or watch royal events like the Changing of the Guard. In addition, London's historic sites like the Tower of London, Westminster Abbey, and St. Paul's Cathedral remain pillars of the city's royal charm.

9. Exciting Day Trips and Excursions
London is perfectly located for easy access to some of England's most beautiful and historic destinations. 2025 presents new ways to enjoy nearby attractions such as Windsor, Bath, and the Cotswolds. Whether you're discovering royal castles, quaint countryside villages, or ancient Roman baths, these day trips provide a perfect complement to your London adventure.

10. A City on the Cutting Edge
London's futuristic skyline is changing with new architectural marvels like The Cheesegrater and The Shard. 2025 also marks the opening of several new urban projects, including the King's Cross redevelopment and the city's enhanced tech and digital hubs. These innovations showcase London's ability to marry old-

world charm with modern design and forward-thinking infrastructure.

11. A City for Every Season

From Christmas markets at Kew Gardens to summer concerts in Hyde Park, London offers a range of experiences that change with the seasons. In 2025, whether you're coming in winter, spring, summer, or fall, there's always a fresh experience awaiting you, from outdoor festivals to holiday light displays, ensuring your trip is tailored to the time of year.

12. London for Families

London is more family-friendly than ever, with new attractions aimed toward children and young travelers. The Science Museum, Natural History Museum, and newly expanded KidZania offer interactive learning experiences, while London's many parks and playgrounds are great for family picnics. Whether you're exploring the city's past or having fun in one of its many child-centric attractions, London offers something for every member of the family.

# CHAPTER 1

## Getting Around London

The transportation system in London is one of the best in the world, which makes it easy for tourists to get around. Here's a short guide to getting around the city like a pro, covering everything from the famous Tube to buses, cars, and more.

1. The London Underground (The Tube)

- A Quick Look: The "Tube," or London Underground, is the city's main public transportation system. Its 11 lines connect the city's main neighborhoods and sites.

- How to Use: To tap in and out at stops, you can buy an Oyster card or use a contactless payment method. The math for each trip is done for you instantly.

- Travel Tips: Avoid peak hours (7:30–9:30 a.m. and 5–7 p.m.) for a more comfortable trip. Remember, elevators follow the "stand on the right, walk on the left" rule.

2. Buses

- Why Choose Buses: London's red double-decker buses are a beautiful way to travel. You can see the city's neighborhoods up close, making it a great choice for first-time tourists.

- Tickets and Payment: Use the same Oyster card or cashless method as the Tube; cash payments are not accepted on buses.

- Top Routes: Routes like the 11 bus pass important sites like Trafalgar Square, Big Ben, and St. Paul's Cathedral, giving you a tour-like experience for a fraction of the cost.

3. Trains and Overground

- When to Use: For longer journeys across Greater London or to explore places beyond the city center, use the Overground or National Rail trains.

- Key Stations: Stations like King's Cross, Victoria, and Paddington are hubs that connect you to popular sites in and outside the city.

4. Taxis and Rideshares

- Black Cabs: London's black taxis are famous and available throughout the city. Fares are metered, and drivers are informed about London's streets.

- Rideshare Options: Companies like Uber are available as well, giving app-based convenience, though rates may vary during high-demand periods.

5. Cycling and Walking

- Cycling: London offers bike rentals via Santander Cycles, with docking points throughout the city. Cycling can be a fast way to discover, especially in bike-friendly zones.

- Walking: Many of London's top sights are clustered together, making walking a useful and enjoyable way to experience the city's history and culture.

6. River Transport

- River Bus Services: River buses are a unique way to move while seeing the Thames. They connect key stops from the London Eye to Greenwich.
- Tickets and savings: Oyster and contactless payments are accepted, with savings for daily caps on fares.

7. Helpful Apps for Navigation

- City mapper: A reliable app for real-time public transport information, trip times, and route planning.

- Transport for London (TfL) Go App: Offers live updates and route maps for navigating all transport modes with ease.

**Key Tips for Efficient Travel**

1. Plan Ahead: Use maps and apps to improve your routes and save time.

2. Avoid Peak Hours: Crowds can be overwhelming; midday travel is usually less congested.

3. Stay Alert for Announcements: Platform and line changes are frequent, especially during maintenance or peak hours.

## Navigating London's Transportation System

Getting around London is easy and quick, thanks to its well-connected public transportation network. Here's a streamlined guide to using the city's transport options with cost-saving tips to make the most of your trip.

**The Tube (London Underground)**

- Overview: The Tube is the quickest way to travel across London's main areas, with lines hitting most major attractions.

- Payment: Use an Oyster card or a smart credit/debit card to pay. Simply tap in and out at spots. Daily fare caps apply, so you won't be charged over a certain amount.
- Cost-Saving Tip: Avoid getting single tickets as they're more expensive. An Oyster card or contactless payment saves greatly per ride.

**Buses**

- Why Choose Buses: Double-decker buses offer a more scenic view of London and are great for short distances.
- Payment: Use the same Oyster or smart card as the Tube. Each trip is charged at a flat rate, with a daily cap if you ride multiple times.
- Cost-Saving Tip: Buses have no "tap out" requirement—just tap in when you board. If you move to another bus within an hour, the second ride is free.

**Trains and Overground**

- When to Use: The Overground and National Rail lines are great for longer trips within Greater London or for getting to areas like Richmond, Greenwich, and other boroughs.
- Payment and Savings: Like the Tube, these accept

Oyster and credit cards. Off-peak prices (usually outside of rush hours) are cheaper.

**Taxis and Rideshares**

- Black Cabs: Reliable, with metered fees. Black cab drivers receive extensive training, so you're in good hands.

- Rideshares: Uber and other app-based services are widely available, though costs can surge during peak hours.

- Cost-Saving Tip: Use rideshares during off-peak hours and check prices on apps to find the best deal.

**River Transport**

- River Buses: Travel along the Thames and see the city from the water. Key stops include the London Eye, Tower of London, and Greenwich.

- Payment: River buses accept Oyster and contactless cards, with savings for off-peak travel.

**Biking and Walking**

- Biking: Santander Cycles (London's public bike rental) is affordable, with bikes offered throughout the city. First 30 minutes are free on every trip.

- Walking: Central London's major landmarks are close together, making walking both a pleasant and practical choice.

**Top Cost-Saving Tips**

1. Daily Fare Caps: Whether on the Tube, bus, or Overground, daily fare caps keep you from overspending.
2. Off-Peak Travel: Traveling after 9:30 a.m. on weekdays or anytime on weekends is cheaper.
3. Kids Travel Free: Children under 11 can travel for free on buses and the Tube with a paid adult.
4. Apps for Navigation: Use Citymapper or the TfL app for real-time updates, route choices, and disruptions.

**Mastering the Tube, Buses, and Trains**

London's Tube, buses, and trains are some of the most efficient ways to explore the city. Here's a quick guide with clear steps to make your experience smooth and hassle-free.

**The Tube (London Underground)**

- Getting Started: The Tube is London's rapid transit system, great for getting across the city quickly.

- How to Pay: Tap in and out with an Oyster card or contactless credit/debit card at the entrance and exit barriers. Avoid getting single tickets as they're more expensive.
- Using the Map: Tube lines are color-coded. Major tourist spots are marked, so it's easy to plan your path. For instance, the Circle line (yellow) goes through major areas like Westminster and Notting Hill.
- Top Tips: - Mind the Gap: Listen for announcements and watch the gap between the train and station.
- Rush Hours: Avoid the Tube from 7-9:30 a.m. and 4:30-7 p.m. for a less crowded experience.

**Buses**

- Why Take the Bus? London's iconic red buses are not only scenic but also cheap. Great for shorter trips and sightseeing.
- How to Pay: Tap in with your Oyster or smart card—no need to tap out. A single price is charged at a flat rate, with a daily cap.
- Routes to Know: - Route 15: Passes the Tower of London, St. Paul's Cathedral, and Trafalgar Square.

- Route 11: Runs by Westminster Abbey, Big Ben, and Buckingham Palace.

- Cost-Saving Tips: With the "Hopper Fare," you can switch buses within an hour for free.

**Trains (Overground and National Rail)**

- When to Use: Ideal for traveling to Greater London or nearby sites like Greenwich, Richmond, and Hampton Court Palace.

- How to Pay: Tap in and out using Oyster or contactless at Overground stops. For National Rail journeys, check if your location is covered by Oyster before you tap in.

- Peak vs. Off-Peak: Off-peak travel is less expensive—try to travel after 9:30 a.m. on weekdays to save.

**Quick Step-by-Step Summary**

1. Plan Your Route: Use apps like Citymapper or Google Maps for the best choices across the Tube, buses, and trains.

2. Tap In & Out: Always tap your Oyster or contactless card at entry and exit places for the Tube and trains. For buses, only tap when boarding.

3. Daily Caps: Once you hit the daily cap, you won't be charged more, making it affordable to explore all day.

4. Avoid Peak Hours: Off-peak hours are less crowded and cheaper, making your trip more enjoyable.

## Biking, Walking, and Eco-Friendly Options

London offers fantastic eco-friendly alternatives for tourists looking to explore while keeping a minimal carbon footprint. Biking, walking, and other green choices make sightseeing enjoyable, scenic, and sustainable.

### Biking Around London

- Rent a Bike: Use Santander Cycles, London's public bike-sharing program. Bikes are available at docking points across the city, with rentals starting as low as £2.

- Top Scenic Routes:

- The Thames Path: Cycle along the river, with stunning views of sites like the Tower Bridge, London Eye, and Tate Modern.

- Hyde Park to Kensington Gardens: Enjoy a relaxed ride through London's famous parks, with natural beauty all around.

- Bike Safety Tips: Use designated bike lanes where possible, wear a helmet, and stay aware of pedestrians and vehicles.

**Walking Tours and Scenic Paths**

- Why Walk? London's compact neighborhoods make it great for walking. Strolling allows you to find hidden gems, charming side streets, and beautiful architecture.

- Best Walking Areas: - South Bank: Walk along the Thames, past the Globe Theatre, Millennium Bridge, and the London Eye.

- Notting Hill: Famous for its colorful houses and the Portobello Road Market, ideal for a leisurely, picturesque walk.

- Westminster to Trafalgar Square: A classic walk through famous sites like Big Ben, Westminster Abbey, and Buckingham Palace.

Eco-Friendly Options

- Electric Scooters: Available for rent in select zones, e-scooters are a fast, eco-friendly choice. Check out Lime and Dott for app-based renting.

- Electric Black Cabs: London's famous black cabs now include electric options, giving a green twist on a classic experience.

- River Boats: Use the Thames Clippers for a scenic, environmentally-friendly river route to many top sites.

**Quick Eco-Friendly Travel Tips**

1. Choose Public Bikes and Scooters: Easy to rent and dock around the city.

2. Plan Scenic Walks: Embrace the city's charm on foot, especially in central areas.

3. Go Electric: Opt for electric cars and riverboats to explore sustainably.

## Tips for Efficient and Stress-Free Travel

Traveling around London can be a breeze if you plan ahead and avoid the usual pitfalls. Here are insider tips to help you explore the city comfortably and stress-free.

1. Avoid Rush Hour

- Peak Times: The Tube, buses, and trains are busy from 7:30 AM to 9:30 AM and 4:30 PM to 6:30 PM. If possible, plan your journey outside these hours to avoid overcrowded trains and long queues.

- Mid-Morning or Late Afternoon: Travel after the morning rush (10 AM–12 PM) or before evening rush hour (3 PM–4:30 PM) for a more relaxed journey.

2. Use Contactless Payments

- Tap in and Out: Use an Oyster card or contactless payment methods (like a debit/credit card or mobile app) for quick entry to public transportation. This eliminates the need to buy paper tickets and helps you avoid long queues.

- Daily Caps: If you're using contactless payment, London automatically uses daily caps, saving you money if you use public transport multiple times.

3. Stay in Central Zones

- Accommodation Tips: Stay within Zones 1 or 2 for easy access to major attractions, restaurants, and transportation hubs. The closer you are to downtown London, the easier it is to avoid long commutes and enjoy more spontaneous adventures.

4. Use the Uber Boat or Thames Clippers

- River Travel: Beat the traffic and enjoy a beautiful trip by taking the Uber Boat or Thames Clippers along the Thames River. It's a relaxing and less crowded way to get around, with stops at major sites.

5. Download Transport Apps

- Plan Your Route: Use apps like Citymapper or Google Maps to check real-time transport changes, plan your route, and avoid delays. These apps will also help you find options if there's an unexpected disruption to your route.

6. Pack Light

- Travel Comfortably: Avoid dragging heavy bags through busy stops or crowded buses. Pack light to make your trip smoother, especially on the Tube or while transferring between stations.

**Bonus Tip: Walk When Possible**

- London is incredibly walkable, and many of the best sights are within walking distance of each other. Not only will you avoid the hassle of public transport, but you'll also get a chance to see the secret gems of the city at your own pace.

# CHAPTER 2

## Where to Stay in London

Finding the right place to stay in London is key to making your visit enjoyable and stress-free. Whether you're after luxury, convenience, or a more budget-friendly choice, London offers a variety of accommodations to suit all preferences.

1. Best Areas to Stay in London

- West End (Covent Garden, Soho, Theatre District): Ideal for theater fans, nightlife enthusiasts, and those who want to be in the heart of the action. You'll be close to top sites like the British Museum, Buckingham Palace, and Covent Garden markets.

- South Bank: Great for families and culture seekers. The area gives iconic views of the Thames and is home to attractions like the London Eye, Tate Modern, and Shakespeare's Globe.

- Kensington & Chelsea: A refined, upscale area great for museum-goers and those who enjoy high-end shopping and dining. The Victoria & Albert Museum and Kensington Gardens are here.

- Shoreditch & East End: The go-to place for art lovers, hipsters, and young travelers. Expect trendy bars, street art, and a lively nighttime scene. Close to Brick Lane and the lively Spitalfields Market.

2. Types of Accommodation

- Luxury Hotels: If you're looking for a lavish stay, try places like The Ritz, Claridge's, or The Dorchester. These hotels offer world-class service, fine dining, and prime sites.

- Boutique Hotels: Smaller and often more unique, boutique hotels such as The Zetter Townhouse or The Hoxton offer stylish, private stays with a local flavor.

- Budget Hotels and Hostels: London has many budget-friendly choices without sacrificing comfort. Look into Premier Inn, Travelodge, or hostels like YHA London Central for cheap stays.

- Vacation Rentals: For those seeking more privacy or a longer stay, sites like Airbnb offer a wide range of rentals, from chic apartments in Shoreditch to cozy flats in Notting Hill.

3. Staying Close to Transport

- Central Locations: Staying near a Tube station is important for getting around easily. Areas like King's Cross, Liverpool Street, and Paddington offer great connection to the entire city.

- Airports: If you're coming from Heathrow, Gatwick, or Stansted, staying near an airport (like the Hilton at Heathrow) can save time, especially for early flights or late arrivals.

4. Short-Term Rentals for Longer Stays

- Airbnb & VRBO: If you're planning a longer stay, these services provide choices for fully furnished apartments, giving you a home-like atmosphere and more freedom to explore.

5. Family-Friendly Stays

- Family Suites: Many hotels in central places offer family suites that cater to groups. Hotels like the Park Plaza Westminster Bridge offer larger rooms for families and easy access to major sites.

- Family-Friendly Neighborhoods: Areas like Bloomsbury and Kensington are great for families, as they offer safe surroundings and easy access to parks, museums, and family activities like the Science Museum.

6. Unique & Unconventional Stays

- Historic Hotels: Stay in a piece of London's history at places like The Tower Hotel, facing the Tower of London, or the charming Brown's Hotel, one of the oldest in the city.

- River Cruises & Floating Hotels: For something different, try a floating hotel or home. Stay on the Thames for unforgettable views and unique adventures.

Bonus Tip: Book in Advance

- London is a busy city year-round, and accommodations fill up fast, especially during peak tourist seasons or big events like Wimbledon or the London Fashion Week. Book your stay well in advance to secure the best deals and the ideal spot.

## Accommodation Options for Every Budget

London offers a wide array of accommodation options to fit any budget. From cheap hostels to luxurious hotels, there's something for everyone. Here's a breakdown of budget, mid-range, and luxury stays with pros and cons to help you choose the best choice for your needs.

1. Budget Stays

Options: Hostels, Budget Hotels, and Airbnb.

**Pros:** - Affordable rates, ideal for tourists who want to save money.

- Many hostels offer a social atmosphere, making it easy to meet fellow tourists.

- Budget hotels like Travelodge or Premier Inn give comfort without the high price tag.

- Airbnb choices offer unique, local stays and often come with kitchen facilities for cooking meals.

**Cons:** - Smaller rooms and shared areas in hostels may lack privacy.

- Locations can sometimes be further from major attractions.

- Basic amenities and fewer fancy features.

Best For: Backpackers, solo travelers, or those wanting to spend most of their time exploring outside the hotel.

2. Mid-Range Stays

Options: 3-4 Star Hotels, Boutique Hotels, and Guesthouses.

**Pros:** - A balance of comfort, ease, and price. - Located in great areas near attractions and transport links. - Offer extra amenities like workout centers, room service, and stylish decor.

- Mid-range chains like Hotel Indigo or CitizenM give modern design and high-end services at a more affordable price point.

**Cons:** - Can still be pricey during peak seasons or in central locations. - Some boutique hotels may have fewer facilities compared to bigger hotels.

Best For: Couples, small families, or visitors who want a comfortable and stylish stay without breaking the bank.

3. Luxury Stays

Options: 5-Star Hotels, High-End Boutique Hotels, and Iconic London Landmarks.

**Pros:** - Premium service, spacious rooms, and top-tier amenities. - Prime locations in central London near major landmarks like Buckingham Palace or the Tower of London. - Luxurious extras such as spas, fine dining, and

24-hour concierge service. - Some hotels like The Ritz, Claridge's, and The Dorchester offer historical charm and timeless elegance.

**Cons:** - Expensive rates, especially during peak trip seasons.

- Some high-end hotels may feel distant or lack a local touch.

Best For: Those wanting a lavish experience with exceptional service, privacy, and convenience.

## Best Neighborhoods to Stay Based on Interests

London is made up of diverse neighborhoods, each giving its own vibe and appeal. Depending on your interests, here are the top places to consider for your stay:

1. Historic & Cultural Vibe: Covent Garden & Westminster

- Covent Garden: Known for its rich history, theaters, and street performances, this area is great for culture lovers. With iconic landmarks like the Royal Opera House and the British Museum nearby, it's an ideal spot for those wanting to be immersed in London's artistic history.

- Westminster: Home to famous sites like Buckingham Palace, the Houses of Parliament, and Westminster Abbey, this area is a must for history enthusiasts. Stay here for easy access to the city's most iconic historic sites.

2. Foodie Haven: Shoreditch & Borough Market

- Shoreditch: The go-to spot for foodies wanting trendy cafes, street food markets, and innovative restaurants. This area is vibrant and packed with eclectic food choices, from artisan coffee shops to world-class dining experiences.

- Borough Market: Situated near London Bridge, Borough Market is a paradise for food fans. This historic market offers a range of fresh produce, artisanal goods, and street food from around the world, all within walking distance of famous landmarks like the Shard.

3. Family-Friendly: South Kensington & Notting Hill

- South Kensington: A family favorite, South Kensington is home to some of London's most family-friendly sites, including the Natural History Museum, Science Museum, and Kensington Gardens. It offers a quieter, more relaxed atmosphere, great for families with children.

- Notting Hill: Famous for its colorful streets and the iconic Portobello Road Market, Notting Hill provides a family-friendly vibe with charming cafes, independent bookstores, and plenty of green places like Holland Park for kids to enjoy.

4. Luxury & Trendy: Mayfair & Chelsea

- Mayfair: A chic and affluent area, Mayfair is home to luxury boutiques, high-end restaurants, and exclusive members-only clubs. Perfect for those who want to indulge in luxury and enjoy proximity to Green Park and Hyde Park.

- Chelsea: With its upscale ambiance, Chelsea is great for fashion-forward travelers. Known for designer shops, trendy cafes, and a stylish crowd, this area oozes elegance, especially around King's Road and Sloane Square.

5. Quirky & Artistic: Camden & Soho

- Camden: Known for its alternative culture, Camden is great for those who love quirky shops, vintage markets, and live music venues. It's a great spot for an edgy, creative vibe with an eclectic mix of bars, cafes, and street art.

- Soho: Soho is the heart of London's nightlife, brimming with lively pubs, trendy restaurants, and creative arts venues. Ideal for those who enjoy a bustling, energetic atmosphere with a mix of culture, food, and nightlife.

6. Relaxed & Green: Hampstead & Richmond

- Hampstead: For a quieter, more suburban feel, Hampstead offers beautiful parks like Hampstead Heath, lovely streets, and a village-like atmosphere. It's great for travelers who prefer a more relaxed environment with easy access to central London.

- Richmond: Situated along the River Thames, Richmond is a peaceful and scenic neighborhood, great for nature lovers. Explore the Richmond Park and enjoy riverside walks, making it a great choice for those wanting a slower-paced, green break from the city.

## Accessibility-Friendly Lodging Choices

London is committed to offering inclusive travel experiences, with various accommodation options that cater to guests with mobility needs. Here are some top choices with important accessibility features:

1. Premier Inn London

- Location: Multiple locations across London, including key places like King's Cross and South Bank.

- Accessibility Features: Premier Inn offers a range of accessible rooms equipped with wider doorways, grab bars, and low-level beds for ease of entry. Some rooms also offer roll-in showers and step-free entry. Many homes have accessible lifts and are wheelchair-friendly.

- Additional Amenities: Accessible parking, assistance with check-in, and staff trained in offering support for guests with mobility challenges.

2. The Nadler Victoria

- Location: Located near Buckingham Palace, Westminster, and Victoria Station.

- Accessibility Features: The Nadler Victoria offers accessible rooms with well-designed bathrooms that include roll-in showers, lowered sinks, and handrails. The rooms have enough space for maneuvering a wheelchair easily.

- Additional Amenities: All public places, including the

reception and restaurant, are wheelchair accessible. They also offer services like mobility scooter rentals upon request.

3. Park Plaza Westminster Bridge London

- Location: In the heart of London, close to the London Eye, Big Ben, and the Houses of Parliament.

- Accessibility Features: The hotel offers accessible rooms with features like wide doors, lowered light switches, roll-in tubs, and emergency pull cords. Bathrooms are equipped with grab rails, and there is step-free entry throughout the hotel. - Additional Amenities: Accessible elevators, accessible parking spots, and concierge services for guests with mobility needs.

4. CitizenM London Bankside

- Location: A short walk from Tate Modern and the Southbank Centre. - Accessibility Features: CitizenM offers roomy, modern rooms with accessible bathrooms that include roll-in showers and handrails. The hotel's design ensures that rooms are equipped with bigger walkways and easy-to-reach amenities.

- Additional Amenities: The hotel has accessible doors, lifts, and is wheelchair-friendly. Staff are attentive to special needs, and accessible parking is provided on request.

5. The Z Hotel Shoreditch

- Location: Situated in the trendy Shoreditch area, known for its artsy vibe and close to public transport links.
- Accessibility Features: The Z Hotel Shoreditch offers accessible rooms with low-level beds, wide doors, and bathrooms with roll-in showers and grab bars.
- Additional Amenities: The hotel's ground-floor services, including reception and dining areas, are wheelchair accessible. Some rooms also offer extra space for ease of movement.

6. Holiday Inn London – Kensington Forum

- Location: A short distance from Kensington Gardens, the Natural History Museum, and the Victoria and Albert Museum.

- Accessibility Features: The Holiday Inn offers accessible rooms with big bathrooms that include step-free showers, grab rails, and emergency call systems. Rooms have wide doorways and sufficient room to maneuver a wheelchair.

- Additional Amenities: The hotel is equipped with accessible lifts and public areas that are intended to accommodate all guests, including those with mobility challenges.

7. St. Pancras Renaissance Hotel London

- Location: Located near St. Pancras International Station, ideal for travelers coming via Eurostar.

- Accessibility Features: The St. Pancras Renaissance Hotel offers accessible rooms with wheelchair-friendly layouts, large bathrooms with roll-in showers, and handrails. The hotel has ramps and lifts for easy entry to all areas.

- Additional Amenities: Accessible parking and concierge services for guests with mobility needs, along with easy transport links to key sites.

8. DoubleTree by Hilton Hotel London – Westminster

- Location: Located near Westminster Abbey and the River Thames.

- Accessibility Features: DoubleTree offers rooms with features such as accessible bathrooms with roll-in tubs, grab bars, and adjustable-height beds. Many rooms also offer easy-to-use settings for light and temperature.

- Additional Amenities: The hotel has step-free access to all main areas, and accessible parking is provided. Staff are trained to help guests with mobility impairments.

# CHAPTER 3

## Top Attractions and Must-Sees

London is a city filled with world-famous landmarks, rich history, and unique experiences. Whether you're a first-time visitor or returning to explore more, these top sites should be at the top of your list.

1. The British Museum

- Why Visit: One of the world's best museums, housing over 8 million works from across history and cultures.

- Highlights: The Rosetta Stone, Egyptian mummies, the Elgin Marbles, and the Assyrian lion hunt reliefs.

- Insider Tip: Admission is free, but booking tickets in advance is suggested for popular exhibits.

2. The Tower of London

- Why Visit: Dive into London's turbulent past, from royal palace to prison and treasury.

- Highlights: The Crown Jewels, Beefeaters (Yeoman Warders), and the Medieval White Tower.

- Insider Tip: Arrive early to avoid crowds and take a guided tour for fascinating historical information.

3. Buckingham Palace

- Why Visit: Home to the British monarch and a symbol of British history.

- Highlights: The Changing of the Guard ceremony, the royal grounds, and the State Rooms (when open to the public).

- Insider Tip: The Changing of the Guard is free to watch and happens daily during summer.

4. The Houses of Parliament and Big Ben

- Why Visit: Iconic landmarks in the heart of London, offering both political importance and stunning architecture.

- Highlights: The clock tower (Big Ben), the House of Commons, and the grand Westminster Hall.

- Insider Tip: Book a guided walk of the Parliament to learn about its history and workings.

5. The London Eye - Why Visit: Experience panoramic views of London from one of the world's biggest observation wheels.

- Highlights: 360-degree views of the city, including St. Paul's Cathedral, The Shard, and the River Thames.

- Insider Tip: Book tickets in advance to skip long queues, especially in peak seasons.

6. The Tate Modern

- Why Visit: A must-see for art lovers, housing modern works in a former power station.
- Highlights: Works by Picasso, Warhol, and Hockney, plus rotating shows.
- Insider Tip: Admission is free for the permanent collection, but temporary displays require a ticket.

7. Covent Garden

- Why Visit: A lively place known for shopping, dining, and street performances.
- Highlights: Market stalls, luxury shops, and the Royal Opera House.
- Insider Tip: Visit in the evening for live entertainment and a vibrant scene.

8. The Natural History Museum - Why Visit: A family favorite with interesting exhibits about the natural world.
- Highlights: The dinosaur skeletons, the giant blue whale model, and the volcano show.

- Insider Tip: The museum is free, but certain shows may have a small charge. Arrive early to escape long lines.

9. Hyde Park - Why Visit: One of London's largest and most beautiful green spaces, great for a leisurely stroll or picnic.

- Highlights: Serpentine Lake, Speaker's Corner, and Kensington Gardens.

- Insider Tip: Rent a bike or boat to explore the park at your own pace.

10. The Shard - Why Visit: The tallest building in Western Europe, giving breathtaking views of London.

- Highlights: Observation decks on the 68th, 69th, and 72nd floors with unrivaled views of the city.

- Insider Tip: Visit at sunset for the most dramatic views as the city lights come to life.

11. Camden Market - Why Visit: A bustling market selling alternative fashion, unique foods, and quirky souvenirs.

- Highlights: Vintage clothes, street food from around the world, and live music.

- Insider Tip: Explore the nearby area, including Camden Lock, for even more hidden gems.

12. St. Paul's Cathedral

- Why Visit: A beautiful Baroque church that is a symbol of resilience, famously surviving the London Blitz.
- Highlights: The Whispering Gallery, the dome, and the crypt.
- Insider Tip: Climb to the top for a panoramic view of London's city

## Iconic Landmarks and When to Visit

London is home to numerous famous landmarks. To make the most of your experience, timing your visit is key to avoiding crowds and maximizing pleasure. Here's a guide to must-see places and the best times to visit them.

1. The Tower of London

- Best Time to Visit: Early morning or late afternoon, especially on weekdays.
- Why: Fewer visitors and cooler temps make for a more pleasant experience. Weekends can get busy.

2. Buckingham Palace

- Best Time to Visit: Early morning before the Changing of the Guard or late afternoon.

- Why: Crowds gather for the event, so visit early for a quieter view or later for fewer tourists in the area.

3. The London Eye

- Best Time to Visit: Right before sunset.

- Why: You'll catch both daily and nighttime views of the city as the lights come on. The evening is usually less crowded.

4. The Houses of Parliament and Big Ben

- Best Time to Visit: Early morning or late evening.

- Why: The area around Westminster is less busy in the morning and evening, giving you the chance to snap pictures without the crowds.

5. St. Paul's Cathedral

- Best Time to Visit: Early morning, around opening time (8:30 AM).

- Why: Avoid the noon rush of tourists. Early visits give time to explore the Whispering Gallery and the dome with fewer visitors.

6. The Shard

- Best Time to Visit: Sunset or early evening.

- Why: Experience breathtaking views as the city transforms from daylight to night, and the crowds are usually smaller during this time.

7. Covent Garden

- Best Time to Visit: Early weekday mornings or late nights.

- Why: Beat the crowds while enjoying the street acts and boutique shops. The market gets very busy around lunch and on weekends.

8. The British Museum - Best Time to Visit: Mid-morning on Tuesdays.

- Why: The museum is less busy before noon and during the week. Weekends and state holidays are much busier.

9. Hyde Park - Best Time to Visit: Early mornings or late afternoons.

- Why: The park is most peaceful early in the morning before runners and tourists arrive or late in the afternoon when the crowds thin out.

10. Camden Market - Best Time to Visit: Early weekday mornings or late afternoons.

- Why: The market is at its busiest on weekends, so coming during the weekdays or after the lunch rush gives you a more relaxed experience.

Timing your visits to London's famous landmarks is all about balancing the must-see experiences with peaceful moments of discovery. By avoiding peak hours, you can explore these places at your own pace and truly soak in all the city has to offer.

## World-Class Museums and Galleries

London is home to an unparalleled collection of world-class museums and galleries, showing art, history, and culture from across the globe. Whether you're an art enthusiast, history buff, or simply looking to explore the city's rich cultural heritage, these institutions offer something for everyone. Here's a quick guide to the top spots and the must-see shows.

1. The British Museum - Why Visit: One of the world's best museums, offering a vast collection that spans millennia of human history.

- Must-See Exhibit: The Rosetta Stone – The key to deciphering ancient Egyptian hieroglyphs, an iconic artifact of immense historical importance.

- Best Time to Visit: Weekdays, mid-morning for a quieter atmosphere.

2. The National Gallery - Why Visit: Home to an incredible collection of European works from the 13th to the 19th centuries.

- Must-See Exhibit: The Arnolfini Portrait by Jan van Eyck and Sunflowers by Vincent van Gogh.

- Best Time to Visit: Early mornings during weekdays or later in the evening when it's less busy.

3. Tate Modern - Why Visit: The UK's premier modern art museum housed in a former power station, showing groundbreaking contemporary art.

- Must-See Exhibit: The Unilever Series – site-specific works in the Turbine Hall by world-renowned artists.

- Best Time to Visit: Weekdays, early afternoon for fewer tourists.

4. Victoria and Albert Museum (V&A) - Why Visit: A stunning collection of art, design, and fashion from across the ages.

- Must-See Exhibit: The Fashion Gallery – An ever-changing exhibit showing fashion and costume through the ages.

- Best Time to Visit: Weekdays, early afternoon to avoid the busy times.

5. The Natural History Museum - Why Visit: A choice for families and science enthusiasts, this museum offers a fascinating glimpse into the natural world.

- Must-See Exhibit: The Dinosaur Gallery – Home to an amazing collection of dinosaur fossils, including a full-size replica of a T. rex.

- Best Time to Visit: Early mornings, especially on weekdays, for a quieter atmosphere.

6. The Science Museum - Why Visit: A dynamic and interactive museum showing the wonders of science and innovation.

- Must-See Exhibit: The Apollo 10 Command Module – Experience the historic space race with this classic exhibit.

- Best Time to Visit: Weekdays, late mornings when the people are fewer.

7. The National Portrait Gallery - Why Visit: Dedicated to portraits of important British figures, it offers insight into the history of the UK through art.

- Must-See Exhibit: The Tudor Gallery – Featuring images of the royal family, including Henry VIII and Elizabeth I.

- Best Time to Visit: Late afternoons or weekdays to avoid crowds.

8. The Design Museum - Why Visit: Focusing on contemporary design, from architecture to fashion, this museum is great for design lovers.

- Must-See Exhibit: Designs of the Year – A yearly exhibit showing the best new designs in all categories.

- Best Time to Visit: Early afternoons on weekdays.

9. The Saatchi museum - Why Visit: A contemporary art museum that often hosts emerging and avant-garde artists.

- Must-See Exhibit: The Saatchi Collection – A regularly updated collection showing cutting-edge contemporary works.

- Best Time to Visit: Weekdays, early afternoon.

10. The Courtauld Gallery - Why Visit: Known for its exquisite collection of Impressionist and Post-Impressionist works.

- Must-See Exhibit: The Sick Child by Edvard Munch and Self Portrait with Cropped Hair by Frida Kahlo.
- Best Time to Visit: Mornings or late afternoons during weekdays for a less busy experience.

## Unique London Tours for an Insider's View

To truly discover London's hidden gems and experience the city beyond the typical tourist spots, consider taking a unique tour that provides insider knowledge, exclusive access, and a deeper connection with the city's rich history and lively culture. Here are some must-try tours that will give you a unique London experience:

1. Jack the Ripper Walking Tour - Why Go: Dive into the wonder and intrigue of London's dark past with a spine-chilling walking tour of the East End. Explore the eerie

streets where Jack the Ripper's gruesome crimes took place and hear the spooky tales from expert guides.

- What to Expect: Visit crime scenes, hear fascinating details about the victims and the investigation, and gain insight into Victorian London's social and cultural background.

- Best For: History buffs, real crime enthusiasts, and thrill-seekers.

2. Secret London VIP Tour - Why Go: Skip the crowds and get exclusive access to some of London's most iconic sites with a VIP experience. This tour takes you beyond the typical sites and offers private visits to hidden spots only locals know about.

- What to Expect: VIP access to sites such as the Tower of London, Buckingham Palace, and Westminster Abbey, often with little to no waiting time. Your expert guide will share personal stories and local tips to make your visit truly special.

- Best For: First-time visitors looking for a luxury experience or those wanting a deeper dive into the city's most famous spots.

3. Harry Potter Studio Tour - Why Go: Immerse yourself in the magical world of Harry Potter with a behind-the-scenes look at the making of the films. From the Great Hall to Diagon Alley, the Warner Bros. Studio Tour gives a fascinating journey through the wizarding world.

- What to Expect: See real sets, props, costumes, and special effects used in the films. Learn about the film-making process and interact with interactive exhibits to experience the magic directly.

- Best For: Harry Potter fans, families, and anyone interested in film history.

4. London Food Tour: A Taste of Borough Market - Why Go: Taste your way through one of London's most iconic food markets. Borough Market is famous for its diverse food scene, offering everything from artisanal cheeses to street food from around the world.

- What to Expect: Guided by a local food expert, explore the market's stalls, try fresh produce, and savor iconic British dishes such as fish and chips, along with foreign flavors that reflect London's multicultural makeup.

- Best For: Food lovers, culinary fans, and anyone looking to experience the city's rich food culture.

5. London's Hidden Gardens Walking Tour - Why Go: Escape the hustle and bustle of the city with a relaxing walk through London's secret gardens. These peaceful getaways are hidden in plain sight, tucked away in courtyards, rooftops, and along quiet streets.

- What to Expect: Explore serene green spaces like the Kyoto Garden in Holland Park and the Roof Gardens in Kensington, led by a passionate horticulturist who will share the history and beauty of each spot.

- Best For: Nature lovers, photography fans, and those looking to unwind.

6. Street Art Tour of Shoreditch - Why Go: Discover the creative side of London with a street art walk through the vibrant neighborhood of Shoreditch. This area is a canvas for some of the world's most renowned street artists, including Banksy, and offers a fresh take on urban art.

- What to Expect: Visit the streets and alleys where stunning murals and graffiti tell stories of political action, culture, and creativity. Your guide will explain the significance of each piece and present you to local artists.

- Best For: Art fans, photographers, and those looking to see an unconventional side of London.

7. Royal London Tour - Why Go: Explore the royal landmarks and history of London, including the grand palaces, stunning parks, and interesting royal history that have shaped the city's character.

- What to Expect: Visit Buckingham Palace, the Changing of the Guard event, Kensington Palace, and St. James's Park. Learn about the British monarchy's legacy from expert guides and watch the royal rituals up close.

- Best For: History lovers, fans of the royal family, and anyone wanting a regal experience.

8. Themed London Pub Tour - Why Go: Discover London's vibrant pub culture and its rich past with a themed pub crawl. Explore historic taverns, hidden speakeasies, and cozy local spots while learning about the city's unique drinking customs.

- What to Expect: Enjoy pints of local ales, taste classic British pub snacks, and hear stories about the pubs' historical importance, from famous authors to political events.

- Best For: Social drinkers, history buffs, and those looking to engage themselves in local culture.

9. Nighttime Photography trip - Why Go: Capture the beauty of London after dark with a guided photography trip. The city's landmarks and streets transform in the glow of streetlights and neon signs, giving the perfect chance for stunning nighttime shots.

- What to Expect: A professional photographer will guide you to the best spots for capturing iconic landmarks like the Tower Bridge, Big Ben, and the London Eye, while giving tips and techniques to get the perfect shot.

- Best For: Photography enthusiasts and anyone looking to see the city in a new light.

10. The London Ghost Walk - Why Go: Explore the spooky side of London with a ghost walk that takes you to the city's most haunted spots. Learn about the eerie tales of murder, mystery, and the supernatural that have become woven into London's past.

- What to Expect: A guided walk through ancient streets, graveyards, and hidden spots where ghostly legends and paranormal encounters have been reported. Perfect for a spine-tingling night out.

- Best For: Thrill-seekers, history fans, and those intrigued by the supernatural.

.

# CHAPTER 4

## Off-the-Beaten-Path London

London is brimming with iconic sites and well-trodden tourist routes, but if you're looking for a more unique and authentic experience, stepping off the beaten path is where the magic happens. From hidden gardens and quirky neighborhoods to overlooked museums and secret bars, there's a side of London that few tourists ever see. Let's discover some of the city's best-kept secrets.

1. Leadenhall Market

- Why Go: Tucked away in the heart of the City of London, Leadenhall Market is a beautiful Victorian covered market that's often missed by the average tourist. Its cobbled streets, intricate glass roof, and ornate building make it a photographer's dream.

- What to Expect: Stroll through this secret gem for boutique shops, cozy cafes, and traditional pubs. It's a peaceful alternative to the crowds of Covent Garden, giving a taste of London's historic charm and a perfect spot to pause and people-watch.

- Best For: Architecture enthusiasts, shopping lovers, and those wanting a quieter, atmospheric experience.

2. Little Venice

- Why Go: Escape the chaos of the city and find peace along the picturesque canals of Little Venice. This peaceful neighborhood, often referred to as London's own Venice, is filled with houseboats, bars, and charming canal-side walks.

- What to Expect: Wander along the waterway, enjoy a scenic boat ride, or grab a coffee at one of the riverside shops. This area offers a calm, nature-filled retreat, great for a leisurely afternoon stroll.

- Best For: Nature lovers, photographers, and anyone looking for a relaxed, scenic spot.

3. God's Own Junkyard

- Why Go: Located in Walthamstow, this vibrant warehouse is a kaleidoscope of neon lights, retro signs, and old movie props. It's a secret gem that offers a fascinating, colorful experience.

- What to Expect: Explore this bright paradise that's part gallery, part museum, and part film studio. The ever-changing display of lights, signs, and artwork is mesmerizing, making it a must-see for art lovers and anyone who respects vibrant, quirky spaces.

- Best For: Art and photography fans, vintage lovers, and anyone looking for a unique, Instagram-worthy experience.

4. The Seven Dials

- Why Go: A stone's throw from Covent Garden, The Seven Dials is a charming area full of independent shops, chic cafes, and secret alleyways. It's often ignored in favor of its more famous neighbors, but it's one of the city's most delightful corners.

- What to Expect: Spend an afternoon wandering the narrow streets, popping in and out of quirky shops, and stopping for a coffee at one of the cool local cafes. The area has a bohemian vibe, with a mix of modern style and historic charm.

- Best For: Shopping enthusiasts, foodies, and anyone looking to discover a hidden London neighborhood.

5. Epping Forest

- Why Go: If you're wanting a day outdoors, Epping Forest is the perfect escape from the city. Located just outside London, this ancient forest offers miles of walking and cycling tracks, beautiful lakes, and an abundance of wildlife.

- What to Expect: Enjoy a peaceful walk through this historic forest, where you'll find fields, woodlands, and tranquil ponds. It's an ideal spot for a picnic, a bike ride, or simply soaking in the natural beauty.

- Best For: Nature lovers, families, and anyone wanting outdoor adventure near London.

6. Daunt Books

- Why Go: Located in Marylebone, Daunt Books is a store that's as much about the experience as it is about the books. Housed in a beautiful Edwardian building with oak-panelled shelves and stunning stained glass windows, it's a must-visit for any book fan.

- What to Expect: Browse through a carefully curated collection of travel books, fiction, and non-fiction. Whether you're looking for your next great read or just a quiet place to sit and browse, Daunt Books offers a serene and atmospheric break from the city bustle.

- Best For: Book lovers, quiet seekers, and anyone in search of a secret literary gem.

7. The Hunterian Museum

- Why Go: Located inside The Royal College of Surgeons, The Hunterian Museum is one of London's most interesting and least-known attractions. It's home to a vast collection of medical specimens, surgical tools, and anatomical models, giving a glimpse into the history of medicine.

- What to Expect: Explore hundreds of rare and intriguing items, from preserved human remains to exotic animal specimens, all displayed in a stunning and historical setting. It's an unorthodox museum experience that's perfect for those wanting something unusual.

- Best For: History buffs, science fans, and anyone with a taste for the curious and the macabre.

8. Camden Passage

- Why Go: Camden Passage is a lovely little street tucked away in Islington. It's a treasure trove of antiques, vintage clothes, and quirky stalls, giving a fantastic escape from

the more commercialized markets of London.
- What to Expect: Spend the day discovering the passage's eclectic mix of antique shops, vintage boutiques, and unique eateries. If you visit on a Wednesday or Saturday, you'll find a busy antiques market full of one-of-a-kind finds.
- Best For: Antique hunters, vintage lovers, and anyone looking to find a hidden shopping street.

9. The Magic Circle

- Why Go: For something truly off the beaten path, experience the world of magic and illusion at The Magic Circle, London's famous club for professional magicians.
- What to Expect: Attend a magic show, watch mesmerizing performances, or even join in a workshop. The Magic Circle offers a personal and mind-bending look at the art of magic in an exclusive setting.
- Best For: Magic fans, anyone looking for an unusual experience, and those seeking to add some surprise to their London trip.

10. The Old Operating Theatre Museum - Why Go: Steeped in history, The Old Operating Theatre is one of

London's oldest medical museums. It's an interesting yet eerie glimpse into Victorian surgical practices and the origins of modern medicine.

- What to Expect: See the preserved operating theatre where patients were once treated without anesthesia, and learn about the tools and techniques used by early doctors. It's a dark yet intriguing museum great for those with an interest in medical history.

- Best For: past enthusiasts, those intrigued by the past of medicine, and anyone looking for a unique and educational experience.

## Hidden Neighborhoods with Local Appeal

London is often defined by its well-known areas like Covent Garden, Soho, and Westminster, but the city also boasts a wealth of lesser-known neighborhoods that offer a more personal, local experience. These hidden gems provide insight into the city's authentic culture and are well worth discovering. From quiet residential streets to vibrant creative hubs, here are some of the most charming and under-the-radar areas in London.

1. Bermondsey - What Makes It Special: Bermondsey is a revitalized riverside neighborhood that's as rich in history as it is in character. Once home to old warehouses and industrial spaces, it has turned into one of London's coolest up-and-coming areas.

- Highlights: Visit the famous Borough Market for artisan food and fresh produce, or head to the Bermondsey Beer Mile to taste craft brews from some of the best local breweries. You can also explore the nearby Southwark Park or check out the modern art scene at the White Cube Gallery.

- Vibe: Hip, trendy, and creative, with a mix of old-world charm and modern flair.

2. Hackney - What Makes It Special: Hackney is the heart of London's alternative society. Once a gritty area, it's now known for its arts scene, creative businesses, and independent spirit. This is where you'll find cutting-edge art galleries, hipster bars, and vintage shops.

- Highlights: Explore Broadway Market on a Saturday for quirky finds and artisan food, visit the Hackney Museum for a glimpse into the area's past, or stroll through the green space of Victoria Park. Don't miss the colorful street art around Hackney Wick.

- Vibe: Edgy, artistic, and youthful, with a creative energy that draws in artists and inventors.

3. Stoke Newington - What Makes It Special: Stoke Newington, or "Stokey" as locals call it, is a peaceful and eclectic neighborhood with a village-like vibe. It offers a quirky mix of independent shops, leafy parks, and cozy bars.

- Highlights: Visit the historic Clissold Park, which features a lovely café, a small animal enclosure, and peaceful green spaces. You can also check out Church Street, lined with vintage shops, independent boutiques, and the famous Abney Park Cemetery.

- Vibe: Relaxed, bohemian, and family-friendly, great for those who enjoy a slower pace of life in the city.

4. Peckham - What Makes It Special: Peckham is a vibrant, multicultural area with a strong sense of community. Known for its street art, lively markets, and great views of the city, it offers a slice of London's creative soul.

- Highlights: Take in panoramic views of London from the Peckham Rye Park or the rooftop bar at Frank's Café. Peckham also has a buzzing culture scene, with venues like the Peckham Pelican and the Bussey Building giving live music, theatre, and independent cinema.

- Vibe: Diverse, creative, and vibrant, with an ever-evolving culture scene and a youthful energy.

5. Crystal Palace - What Makes It Special: Nestled in South London, Crystal Palace is a quiet yet quirky area known for its large park, historical landmarks, and antique shops. Its name comes from the impressive Crystal Palace, which once housed the Great Exhibition of 1851.

- Highlights: Wander around the expansive Crystal Palace Park, home to interesting Victorian-era dinosaur statues and a maze. The area also boasts an array of independent shops, antique stores, and food markets, making it great for a relaxed day out.

- Vibe: Family-friendly, historical, and tranquil, offering a suburban escape with a bit of vintage charm.

6. Camberwell - What Makes It Special: Camberwell is an artistic and culturally diverse area that's often overshadowed by its trendier neighbors, but its lively atmosphere and community spirit make it a true local favorite.

- Highlights: Explore the independent art scene at the Camberwell College of Arts or enjoy the calm surroundings of Burgess Park. The area also offers excellent food spots, ranging from global cuisine to cozy local cafes.

- Vibe: Artsy, multicultural, and laid-back, with a relaxed but lively community.

7. Islington - What Makes It Special: Islington is a mix of traditional London charm and modern luxury. Known for its tree-lined streets, historic pubs, and trendy shops, it offers a slightly more refined, residential feel compared to other places.

- Highlights: Head to Upper Street for its chic shops, restaurants, and theaters, or explore the charming Barnsbury neighborhood with its Georgian architecture.

Don't miss a visit to the beautiful Islington Green or the lively Exmouth Market.

- Vibe: Elegant, trendy, and slightly more upscale, offering a quiet residential vibe with a touch of urban style.

8. Walthamstow - What Makes It Special: Walthamstow is a diverse and up-and-coming neighborhood in East London that combines modern living with rich cultural history. Once known for its industrial areas, it now boasts green places, creative hubs, and a thriving local food scene.

- Highlights: Visit the Walthamstow Market, the longest outdoor market in Europe, or enjoy the tranquil Walthamstow Wetlands for nature walks and birdwatching. The area also features creative places like the God's Own Junkyard, a neon wonderland of art and pop culture.

- Vibe: Eclectic, creative, and community-focused, with a mix of old and new.

9. Shoreditch - What Makes It Special: Shoreditch is an area that constantly reinvents itself, drawing creative

professionals, tech companies, and street artists. Its industrial past has given way to a lively mix of galleries, food markets, and independent shops.

- Highlights: Explore the street art at Brick Lane, visit the Old Truman Brewery for events and markets, or sample food at the famous Boxpark pop-up mall. Shoreditch is also known for its nightlife, with a mix of cool bars, music places, and quirky clubs.

- Vibe: Trendy, artsy, and ever-evolving, with an energetic vibe great for creatives and night owls.

10. Hammersmith - What Makes It Special: Located along the River Thames, Hammersmith offers a unique mix of riverside living, rich history, and cultural offerings. It's often ignored by tourists but offers plenty of charm and local appeal.

- Highlights: Take a walk along the riverbank, visit the historic Hammersmith Bridge, or explore the charming shopping streets of King Street. Hammersmith is also home to the Lyric Theatre and the Eventim Apollo, two of London's top live entertainment venues.

- Vibe: Traditional yet modern, with a mix of quiet riverside walks and vibrant cultural sites.

London's hidden neighborhoods are where the real essence of the city can be found. These places offer a more authentic, off-the-beaten-path experience, showcasing local culture, creativity, and charm. Whether you're seeking history, art, food, or a relaxing escape, these neighborhoods provide something for every visitor looking to experience a different side of London.

## Quirky Attractions You Won't Find on the Usual Lists

London is brimming with well-known sights like the Tower of London, Buckingham Palace, and the London Eye. But for those who crave something a bit offbeat and surprising, the city offers a treasure trove of quirky, unusual experiences that are perfect for adventurous travelers. From hidden gems and unusual museums to unexpected curiosities, here are some of the quirkiest sites that make London an even more exciting city to explore.

1. The Seven Dials - What It Is: A small area in Covent Garden with a history of being a meeting point for thieves and smugglers. Today, it's a vibrant area filled with independent shops, quirky boutiques, and unique eateries.

- Why Visit: This pedestrianized area is home to some of London's most unusual shops, including a store fully dedicated to selling only socks and one specializing in taxidermy. It's an interesting mix of the old and the new.

2. Leadenhall Market - What It Is: A beautiful Victorian market in the heart of the City of London that's often missed by tourists.

- Why Visit: Its stunning building, with cobbled streets and ornate ceilings, makes it one of the most photogenic spots in London. Not only is it great for shopping, but it's also famous as a filming spot for Harry Potter—the entrance to Diagon Alley was filmed here.

3. God's Own Junkyard - What It Is: A bright, kaleidoscopic warehouse full of neon art, signs, and movie props in Walthamstow.

- Why Visit: This bizarre collection of neon signs, movie props, and art pieces creates a visually striking experience. The vibrant colors and eclectic mix of art make it a photographer's dream. It's truly a hidden gem off the usual tourist radar.

4. The Hunterian Museum - What It Is: A museum hidden within the Royal College of Surgeons, showing a collection of medical oddities and curiosities.

- Why Visit: The museum is home to over 3,500 anatomical and pathological exhibits, including human bones, preserved organs, and preserved animals. It's a fascinating and slightly macabre look into the past of medicine.

5. Little Venice - What It Is: A beautiful area in West London known for its scenic canals, often compared to the canals of Venice, Italy.

- Why Visit: Explore the tranquil waterways by taking a canal boat ride from Little Venice to Camden Market, going through charming, tree-lined canals. It's a peaceful escape from the city hustle, with cozy waterside bars and quirky houseboats.

6. The Crypt of St. Martin-in-the-Fields - What It Is: A hidden crypt beneath a historic church in Trafalgar Square that's now home to a café and art store.

- Why Visit: Many visitors don't know that beneath the famous church is a crypt that's been turned into a stunning space for dining and art exhibitions. Enjoy a coffee surrounded by old tombs, or browse the works of local artists in this atmospheric setting.

7. The Old Operating Theatre Museum - What It Is: Located in the attic of St. Thomas' Church, this museum gives a chilling glimpse into London's medical past.
- Why Visit: The museum showcases the tools, instruments, and methods used in early surgery, before anesthesia or antiseptics were found. It's an interesting, though slightly eerie, step back in time for those interested in the history of medicine.

8. The Moomin Shop - What It Is: A shop dedicated to the famous Finnish Moomin characters, located in Covent Garden.

- Why Visit: For fans of Tove Jansson's quirky and whimsical Moomins, this is the place to find an array of merchandise, including toys, books, and homeware. It's a fun, charming spot that stands out in a city known for high-end fashion.

9. The Magic Circle - What It Is: London's private club for magicians, situated near Euston.

- Why Visit: While it's not open to the public, you can book tickets for exclusive shows and events held at The Magic Circle. For a truly magical experience, watch world-class magicians performing close-up magic and illusions in a secret, historic venue.

10. The Shard's "Unusual" Viewing Platform - What It Is: While The Shard is one of London's tallest buildings, its viewing deck offers an unexpected and less touristy experience than other famous views in London.

- Why Visit: Skip the normal "tourist trap" attractions and visit the Shard during off-peak hours for a more peaceful experience. You'll get a 360-degree view of the city that goes out to the farthest edges of London. It's ideal for tourists who want an unparalleled view without the crowds.

11. Epping Forest - What It Is: A vast and ancient forest located just outside London, giving a natural retreat in the midst of the urban landscape.

- Why Visit: The forest covers over 2,400 hectares and is the perfect place for hiking, picnicking, and wildlife watching. It's an oasis of calm, with peaceful woods and secret ponds, offering a stark contrast to the city's fast-paced energy.

12. The Magdalen College Gardens - What It Is: A peaceful, hidden garden found near the banks of the Thames, often overlooked by visitors.
- Why Visit: Tucked behind the famous Magdalen College, this serene garden offers amazing views of the Thames and is a great place to escape the busy city. The park is home to a collection of beautiful flowers, tranquil pathways, and historical monuments.

London's quirky sites provide a refreshing break from the standard sightseeing route. Whether you're interested in eccentric museums, hidden gardens, or unusual historical sites, these offbeat spots give you a deeper, more unique view on the city. So, step off the beaten path and dive into these lesser-known wonders for a truly memorable London journey.

## Local Favorites: Pubs, Cafes, and Secret Gardens

London is known for its buzzing energy, iconic landmarks, and cosmopolitan style. But beneath the hustle and bustle, there's a quieter, more personal side of the city loved by locals. From cozy, hidden pubs tucked away on narrow streets to peaceful secret gardens offering respite from city life, these local favorites provide a slice of London that many tourists miss. Here are some of the best pubs, cafes, and serene spots that capture the true spirit of London.

1. The Churchill Arms (Kensington) - What It Is: A charming, historic pub draped in flowers, serving both a cozy setting and a great selection of beers.

- Why Visit: This pub isn't just known for its Victorian-style exterior—it's also a secret gem for Thai food. The Churchill Arms serves up some of the best Thai dishes in

London, making it a unique place to relax, enjoy a pint, and eat in an unexpected setting.

2. The Ledbury (Notting Hill) - What It Is: A renowned but understated pub, tucked in the heart of Notting Hill, serving exceptional pub food with a cozy and unpretentious environment.

- Why Visit: It's a true neighborhood favorite for its hearty, British fare and laid-back vibe. Perfect for anyone wanting an authentic pub experience that feels like a home away from home. Their roasted meats and classic pies are a must-try.

3. Sketch (Mayfair) - What It Is: A whimsical, artistic cafe and diner that doubles as an art gallery.

- Why Visit: The café's quirky, engaging design makes it a favorite for both locals and tourists. The famous pink room is a popular spot for afternoon tea, while their art shows and eccentric decor provide a one-of-a-kind experience. It's perfect for anyone looking to enjoy both a coffee and some creativity in a relaxed setting.

4. The Barrowboy & Banker (London Bridge) - What It Is: A historic bar near London Bridge known for its

Victorian charm and lively atmosphere.

- Why Visit: With its warm wooden interiors and bustling atmosphere, this bar is the perfect stop after a walk along the Thames. Whether you're in the mood for a refreshing pint or hearty British classics, this pub offers a local experience away from the usual tourist crowds.

5. The Attendant (Farringdon) - What It Is: A former Victorian public toilet turned into a stylish café.

- Why Visit: Don't let the unusual roots fool you—this quirky café is beloved by locals for its strong coffee and trendy vibes. The exposed brick walls and vintage furniture add to the café's charm. It's the right spot for a unique break and a great cup of coffee.

6. God's Own Junkyard Café (Walthamstow) - What It Is: Nestled inside the neon-lit wonderland of God's Own Junkyard, this café serves up bright food amidst an equally colorful atmosphere.

- Why Visit: For a truly Instagrammable experience, pair your coffee with some of London's most unusual neon art. The café serves wonderful cakes and coffee, but the real draw is the eye-popping surroundings. It's the right blend of creativity and comfort.

7. The Roof Gardens (Kensington) - What It Is: A hidden gem atop a building giving stunning views of the city, lush greenery, and a peaceful atmosphere.
- Why Visit: Located above the hustle and bustle of Kensington High Street, The Roof Gardens offers a secluded, tranquil spot for locals to relax. Whether you're having a drink at sunset or simply strolling through its lush gardens, it's a perfect escape from the busy city below.

8. The Queen's Walk Garden (South Bank) - What It Is: A peaceful green space found along the South Bank of the Thames, filled with flowers and plants.
- Why Visit: A hidden oasis along one of London's most lively areas, this secret garden is the perfect spot to take a break from the crowds and enjoy some quiet. The views of the Thames, along with the nearby foliage, make it an ideal place to rest and recharge.

9. The Garden at 120 (Shoreditch) - What It Is: A rooftop garden giving panoramic views of the city's skyline.

- Why Visit: For those who enjoy a unique view on the city, The Garden at 120 is an often-overlooked spot that locals love. It's free to visit and provides fantastic views of the city's famous sites from a peaceful and green vantage point. It's great for taking in the sights while enjoying the fresh air.

10. Kensington Roof Gardens (Kensington) - What It Is: A lush, green rooftop spot offering a café, beautiful views, and a chance to escape the busy streets below.

- Why Visit: This hidden gem allows you to relax in a beautiful, nature-filled setting with views across London. It's a quieter alternative to the more popular parks, great for spending a few hours enjoying nature in the heart of the city.

11. Clerkenwell Green (Clerkenwell) - What It Is: A charming, secret garden tucked between old industrial buildings in one of London's trendiest areas.

- Why Visit: Clerkenwell Green is a peaceful break from the busy streets nearby. With lush trees and benches to sit on, it's great for those looking to enjoy a few quiet moments in an otherwise bustling part of London.

12. The Vaults (Waterloo) - What It Is: A creative space offering everything from immersive theater shows to secret cafes.

- Why Visit: The Vaults' underground position and artistic vibe give it an exclusive, hidden feel. It's a wonderful spot to explore London's creative community and discover underground shows and cozy cafes.

# CHAPTER 5

## Suggested Itineraries

When planning a trip to London, it's easy to feel overwhelmed by the endless options of things to do and see. To help you get the most out of your visit, here are a variety of suggested itineraries, tailored to different hobbies and time frames. Whether you're in London for a weekend, a week, or more, these itineraries offer the perfect mix of iconic landmarks, hidden gems, and local favorites to ensure you make the most of your time in this dynamic city.

1. Classic London in 3 Days

Day 1: Iconic Landmarks - Morning: Start your day with a visit to the Tower of London, where you can explore centuries of history, including the Crown Jewels and the medieval White Tower.

- Afternoon: Walk along the River Thames to Tower Bridge and continue to St. Paul's Cathedral. Don't forget to take a moment to enjoy the views from the Millennium Bridge.

- Evening: End the day with a ride on the London Eye for stunning views of the city's skyline, especially as the lights start to twinkle.

Day 2: Museums and Galleries - Morning: Begin with a visit to the British Museum to view old treasures like the Rosetta Stone and Egyptian mummies.

- Afternoon: Head to Covent Garden for lunch, then explore the National Gallery and Tate Modern to experience world-class art from across the ages.

- Evening: Catch a West End show in the Theatre District, offering a choice of performances from musicals to dramas.

Day 3: Local Neighborhoods - Morning: Take a leisurely walk through Hyde Park and visit Kensington Palace. Then, head to the charming streets of Notting Hill and explore its lively markets and boutique shops.

- Afternoon: Visit the vibrant Camden Market for a mix of food, shopping, and street acts.

- Evening: Experience the lively atmosphere of Soho, with its eclectic mix of bars, restaurants, and entertainment places.

2. Hidden Gems in London (3 Days)

Day 1: Quirky Spots and Hidden History - Morning: Start your day with a visit to God's Own Junkyard in Walthamstow, a fascinating collection of neon art in a former warehouse.

- Afternoon: Wander around Leadenhall Market, one of the city's oldest markets, and then explore The Seven Dials, a charming area filled with independent shops and secret alleys.

- Evening: Head to The Churchill Arms in Kensington for dinner in a pub with an interesting twist—authentic Thai food in a flower-covered Victorian building.

Day 2: Off-the-Beaten-Path Parks and Cafes - Morning: Start with a peaceful walk in Postman's Park, a secret oasis offering a memorial to heroic self-sacrifice.

- Afternoon: Visit the Daunt Books in Marylebone, a bookshop set in an Edwardian building. Then, grab coffee at The Attendant, a quirky café set in a former Victorian toilet.

- Evening: End your day with drinks at The Vaults under

Waterloo Station, where the underground space hosts immersive shows and cozy cafes.

Day 3: Local Markets and Unique Experiences

- Morning: Visit Columbia Road Flower Market (Sunday only) to see one of the city's most lively markets. Explore the surrounding streets filled with local shops and street food stalls.

- Afternoon: Head to Brick Lane for a walk through this eclectic area, known for its street art, vintage shops, and curry houses.

- Evening: Discover Camden Market for dinner, where you can try an array of global cuisines in a laid-back, artsy environment.

3. Family-Friendly London in 2 Days

Day 1: Exploring the Best Family Attractions - Morning: Start your day at the Natural History Museum, where kids will be in awe of the giant dinosaur skeletons and interactive exhibits.

- Afternoon: Head to Hyde Park for a fun family lunch or boat ride on the Serpentine. Then, stop by Princess Diana

Memorial Playground, an amazing play area themed after Peter Pan.

- Evening: Watch a family-friendly show in the West End, such as The Lion King or Matilda the Musical.

Day 2: Zoos, Aquariums, and Interactive Fun - Morning: Visit London Zoo in Regent's Park, home to over 750 species and a variety of animal experiences that will engage and teach kids.

- Afternoon: Explore the SEA LIFE London Aquarium, where children can enjoy getting up close with sharks, penguins, and rays.

- Evening: End the day at Covent Garden, where the whole family can enjoy street performances and a range of fun dining options.

4. 24 Hours in London for First-Timers

Morning: Iconic Sites - Start at Big Ben, the Houses of Parliament, and Westminster Abbey. These iconic sites offer a perfect introduction to the city's past.

- Stroll down Whitehall to Downing Street, and visit Trafalgar Square.

Lunch: Market Dining - Head to Borough Market for lunch, offering a range of gourmet food from British cheeses to freshly made pastries.

Afternoon: Museums and Views - Visit the Tate Modern or National Gallery for some art appreciation.

- Take a river cruise along the Thames to see the city from the water, past landmarks like London Bridge and the Shakespeare's Globe.

Evening: Relax and Dine - End your day with a sunset ride on the London Eye, offering amazing views of the city's landmarks.

- Dine at a cozy pub or trendy restaurant in Soho or Covent Garden, and enjoy the bustling evening.

5. Romantic London in 2 Days

Day 1: Explore London's Most Romantic Spots - Morning: Take a boat ride on the River Thames to Greenwich, visiting the Royal Observatory and standing on the Prime Meridian line.

- Afternoon: Stroll hand-in-hand through St. James's Park, with its beautiful flower beds and swan-filled lake.
- Evening: Enjoy a candlelit dinner at one of London's

romantic restaurants, such as Clos Maggiore in Covent Garden, known for its intimate atmosphere and seasonal food.

Day 2: Secluded Gardens and Scenic Views - Morning: Visit the secluded Chelsea Physic Garden, a peaceful space showing historic plants and garden design.

- Afternoon: Explore the green Hampstead Heath, and take a walk to Parliament Hill for one of the best views of London's skyline.

- Evening: End the trip with a sunset view from Primrose Hill, followed by a cozy evening at a secret bar like The Mayor of Scaredy Cat Town.

## 1, 3, and 5-Day Itineraries for All Interests

No matter how long you have to explore London, there's a great itinerary to fit your schedule. From iconic sites to hidden gems, these itineraries offer the best way to see the city's most important sights, balanced with plenty of opportunities to relax and soak in the local culture. Whether you're here for just a day, a weekend, or a full week, these plans will help you make the most of your time in London.

## 1-Day London Itinerary: Essential Highlights for First-Timers

Morning: Classic London sites - Start at Big Ben and the Houses of Parliament: Begin your day at one of London's most iconic sites. The Houses of Parliament and the Elizabeth Tower (Big Ben) are great for photos and a quick introduction to London's rich history.
- Walk to Westminster Abbey: Just a few minutes away, this ancient church is the site of royal coronations, weddings, and burials. Take a short tour to see its beautiful architecture and learn about its importance.
- Visit Buckingham Palace: A short walk through St. James's Park gets you to Buckingham Palace. Catch the Changing of the Guard event if you're there at the right time.

Lunch: Historic Pubs or Trendy Cafés - Try a traditional British pub: Head to The Churchill Arms or The

Blackfriar for a casual, historic lunch experience, or choose a trendy café in Covent Garden for a lighter bite.

Afternoon: Explore Iconic Sights - The London Eye: After lunch, head to the London Eye for amazing views of the city. It's a great way to spot other sites from above, including St. Paul's Cathedral, the Shard, and Tower Bridge.

- Walk along the South Bank: Take a walk along the South Bank of the River Thames to pass Shakespeare's Globe and Tate Modern, which are both worthy of a brief visit if time allows.

Evening: West End Show or Dinner - Catch a West End Show: London's Theatre District is famous for its world-class shows. From musicals to dramas, choose a show that fits your plan.

- Dine in Covent Garden: Enjoy a meal at one of the many places in Covent Garden. Choose between Michelin-star dining or casual eateries based on your mood.

**3-Day London Itinerary: A Deeper Dive into the City**

Day 1: Iconic Landmarks and Royal History

- Morning: Start with Big Ben, Westminster Abbey, and Buckingham Palace. Spend time exploring the rich history of these sites and the changing of the guard ceremony.

- Afternoon: Visit Trafalgar Square, and then head to the National Gallery for a taste of world-class art. Afterward, take a leisurely walk through St. James's Park.

- Evening: End your day with a ride on the London Eye and a dinner along the South Bank. Consider a riverside spot for a great view of the city skyline at night.

Day 2: Museums and Cultural Hotspots

- Morning: Start the day at the British Museum. Home to everything from the Rosetta Stone to Egyptian mummies, this is one of the world's most famous museums.

- Afternoon: Visit Covent Garden for lunch, then head to The Tate Modern and The Millennium Bridge. Walk to St. Paul's Cathedral for its stunning building and panoramic views from the dome.

- Evening: Have dinner in Soho, known for its lively nightlife and wide range of dining options. Afterward, take in a West End show.

Day 3: Local Neighborhoods and Hidden Gems

- Morning: Start with a visit to Notting Hill and explore its charming streets and the famous Portobello Road Market. Don't miss the quaint shops and street food sellers.

- Afternoon: Head to Camden Market for lunch, where you can try food from around the world. Spend the afternoon browsing the colorful market and checking out local street art.

- Evening: Explore Soho or Shoreditch for dinner and drinks at one of the many trendy spots. End the night with a drink at a speakeasy or rooftop bar for great views.

**5-Day London Itinerary: A Comprehensive London Experience**

Day 1: Iconic Landmarks and Historic Sites - Morning:

Begin at Big Ben, Westminster Abbey, and Houses of Parliament. Spend time soaking in the grandeur of these historical sites.

- Afternoon: Head to Buckingham Palace, then take a relaxing walk through St. James's Park and stop for lunch in the area. Continue your journey to Trafalgar Square and the National Gallery.

- Evening: Take a ride on the London Eye, followed by dinner at a restaurant along the South Bank, where you can enjoy great views of the city's skyline.

Day 2: Museums and Art - Morning: Start at the British Museum to marvel at the world's oldest items. Then, head to Covent Garden for a break and enjoy a coffee or a snack.

- Afternoon: Spend the afternoon at The Tate Modern, Millennium Bridge, and St. Paul's Cathedral.

- Evening: Enjoy dinner at a famous restaurant in the Theatre District, followed by a West End show.

Day 3: Hidden Gems and Quirky Experiences - Morning: Explore Leadenhall Market, then head to Shoreditch for its colorful street art and boutique shopping.

- Afternoon: Visit the quirky God's Own Junkyard in Walthamstow for an art-filled experience, or explore the quiet Kew Gardens for a change of pace.

- Evening: Explore Soho or Shoreditch for dinner at one of the area's unique restaurants or bars.

Day 4: London's Neighborhoods and Markets - Morning: Start in Notting Hill, wander through Portobello Road Market, and explore the lively streets. Grab lunch at a nearby café.

- Afternoon: Visit Camden Market for lunch and enjoy the bustling scene. Browse the interesting shops, art galleries, and food stalls.

- Evening: Experience the vibrant nightlife of Shoreditch or Soho, with trendy bars and restaurants offering a wide range of cuisines.

Day 5: Parks, Views, and Relaxation - Morning: Spend your morning at Hyde Park, visit Kensington Palace, and take a boat ride on the Serpentine.

- Afternoon: Head to Primrose Hill for panoramic views of the city, or take a walk through Regent's Park and visit London Zoo.

- Evening: Enjoy a relaxing dinner at a riverside restaurant or a rooftop bar, giving views of the Thames and the London skyline.

## Seasonal Activities and Events to Plan Around

London offers a range of unique events and experiences throughout the year. Whether you're coming during the vibrant spring, sunny summer, colorful autumn, or festive winter, there's always something special to enjoy. Here's a breakdown of the must-do seasonal events in the city.

**Spring (March to May): Blooming Beauty and Outdoor Fun**

- Visit Kew Gardens in Full Bloom: Spring in London means bright flowers and stunning landscapes, especially at Royal Botanic Gardens, Kew. The gardens are in full bloom, giving a colorful display of plants, flowers, and seasonal exhibitions.

- Enjoy the Chelsea Flower Show (May): One of London's top events, this world-renowned flower show is held every May in Chelsea. It displays stunning garden designs, horticultural innovations, and exotic plant life.

- Take a Boat Ride on the Thames: Spring is the perfect time to enjoy a peaceful boat ride along the Thames. The mild weather and clear skies offer great views of sites like Tower Bridge, Big Ben, and The London Eye.

- Explore Hyde Park and Regent's Park: As the weather warms, spend time in London's famous parks. Hyde Park and Regent's Park are great for leisurely strolls, outdoor picnics, or renting a pedal boat on the Serpentine.

**Summer (June to August): Festival Fever and Outdoor Adventures**

- Attend the BBC Proms (July to September): If you're a fan of classical music, the BBC Proms at the Royal Albert Hall is a must-do summer exercise. This run of concerts includes world-class performances from top musicians.

- Visit Open-Air Markets and events: Summer in London means outdoor events and street food markets. Don't miss Borough Market for fresh produce and foreign cuisine, or check out the Southbank Centre Summer Festivals for art, music, and cultural events.

- Watch Wimbledon (July): If you're in London during the summer, watching a match at Wimbledon is an iconic event. Enjoy the tennis matches and indulge in a classic serving of strawberries and cream.

- Outdoor Cinema and Theatre: London's outdoor cinemas and theatre shows come alive in summer. Check out Regent's Park Open Air Theatre or catch an alfresco movie screening at places like Greenwich or Somerset House.

**Autumn (September to November): Fall Foliage and Cozy Vibes**

- Experience the Autumn Leaves at Hampstead Heath and Hyde Park: The fall foliage in Hampstead Heath and Hyde Park offers beautiful walks among trees dressed in bright oranges, reds, and yellows. It's the perfect time for photography or a peaceful afternoon walk.

- Attend the London Film Festival (October): The BFI London Film Festival is a highlight for film enthusiasts, giving screenings of the latest films from around the world, along with director talks and events.

- Take a Historic Pub Tour: The cooler weather makes fall a great time to explore London's historic pubs. Go on a pub crawl to discover cozy spots like The George Inn and The Blackfriar, which are rooted in history.

**Winter (December to February): Festive Fun and Cozy Comforts**

- Visit Winter Wonderland in Hyde Park (November to January): Hyde Park Winter Wonderland turns into a magical Christmas market, complete with an ice skating rink, carnival rides, and holiday-themed attractions. It's a must-see for children and couples alike.

- Celebrate New Year's Eve with Fireworks: London's New Year's Eve Fireworks show is one of the most iconic in the world. Head to the South Bank or along the Thames for an unbeatable view of the amazing show at midnight.

- Explore Christmas Markets and Shopping: London is magical during the holiday season, with Christmas markets like Southbank Centre Winter Market and Leicester Square Christmas Market offering festive food, gifts, and decorations. Don't forget to check out the famous Christmas lights along Oxford Street and Covent Garden.

- Ice Skating at Somerset House: The Somerset House Ice Rink is one of the best places to skate in London, surrounded by beautiful buildings and stunning festive lights. It's an unforgettable winter adventure.

- Warm Up in Cosy Pubs: Winter is the best time to enjoy London's cozy pubs. Warm up with a pint of British ale or mulled wine at popular spots like The Mayflower in Rotherhithe or The Old Bank of England in the City.

## Themed Itineraries: Royal, Historical, Family-Friendly

London is a city rich in history, culture, and iconic sites, offering something for everyone. Whether you're fascinated by the royal family, eager to dive into the city's past, or wanting a fun, family-oriented experience, there's a themed itinerary tailored just for you. Here's a breakdown of three exciting itineraries, each meant to offer a unique lens on the city.

### Royal Itinerary: A Day in the Life of Royalty

**Morning:** - Buckingham Palace: Begin your royal journey with a visit to Buckingham Palace, the official home of the British monarch. Watch the famous Changing of the Guard event and explore the magnificent palace grounds.

- St. James's Park: Take a leisurely walk through St. James's Park, which offers stunning views of the palace and tranquil walking paths, great for a morning stroll.

**Lunch:** - Head to The Goring Hotel for an indulgent afternoon tea in one of London's most regal settings. This upscale hotel has been a favorite of the royal family for years.

**Afternoon:** - Westminster Abbey: Explore Westminster Abbey, a UNESCO World Heritage site and the usual venue for royal weddings, coronations, and funerals. Don't miss the Poets' Corner and the stunning building.
- Kensington Palace: Spend the afternoon at Kensington Palace, the London home of several royals, including the Duke and Duchess of Cambridge. Explore the beautiful gardens and learn about the royal past of this palace.

**Evening:** - Royal Opera House: End your royal day by watching a performance at the Royal Opera House in Covent Garden. Immerse yourself in a night of world-class music and theater.

**Historical Itinerary: Step Back in Time**

**Morning:** - Tower of London: Start your day with a visit to the Tower of London, one of the city's oldest and most famous sites. Discover the history of the Crown Jewels, the legendary Ravens, and ages of royal intrigue. - Tower Bridge: Walk across the famous Tower Bridge, and enjoy panoramic views of London's skyline and the Thames River. Don't miss the glass-floored walkway for a unique view.

**Lunch:** - Grab a bite at Borough Market, one of London's oldest food markets, offering an array of local and foreign delights.

**Afternoon:** - The British Museum: Dive into London's past with a visit to The British Museum. Explore artifacts covering over two million years of human history, from ancient Egyptian mummies to the Elgin Marbles. - The Houses of Parliament and Big Ben: Take a walk along the Thames and stop by the Houses of Parliament, where you can admire the Big Ben clock tower. If you have time, join an organized tour inside the Parliament to learn about British politics and history

**Evening:** - Museum of London: End your history tour with a visit to the Museum of London. Explore the city's transformation from prehistoric times through the Roman period and into current history.

**Family-Friendly Itinerary: Fun for All Ages**

**Morning:** - Natural History Museum: Start your day with a visit to the Natural History Museum, one of London's most family-friendly sites. Marvel at the dinosaur skeletons, explore the interactive exhibits, and find the wonders of the natural world.

- Hyde Park: After the museum, head to Hyde Park for some outdoor fun. Kids can enjoy the Princess Diana Memorial Playground, a pirate ship-themed playground, or take a ride on the Hyde Park Pedal Boats.

**Lunch:** - Stop for lunch at The Orangery in Kensington Gardens, where you can enjoy a relaxed meal while watching the beautiful surroundings.

**Afternoon:** - London Zoo: Spend the afternoon at the ZSL London Zoo, one of the oldest and most famous zoos in the world. It's home to over 750 kinds of animals and offers fun, educational experiences for children of all ages.

- London Eye: Take a ride on the London Eye, one of the world's biggest observation wheels. The entire family will enjoy amazing 360-degree views of London's landmarks.

**Evening:** - Covent Garden: Explore Covent Garden, where the whole family can enjoy street performances, boutique shopping, and casual dining choices. If you're in the mood for a family-friendly theater experience, check out a show in the West End.

## Budget-Friendly Itinerary Planner

London, a city where history, culture, and modern life intertwine, can be an exciting yet affordable destination. Whether you're traveling with family, friends, or solo, this budget-friendly itinerary will help you discover the best of London without breaking the bank.

### Day 1: Classic Attractions at No Cost

Start your journey with iconic landmarks that won't cost you a penny.

- The British Museum: Discover one of the world's greatest collections of art, history, and culture.

Entry is free, and you can spend hours exploring ancient artifacts from Egypt, Greece, and beyond.

- Trafalgar Square and the National Gallery: The National Gallery has free admission and works by Van Gogh, Leonardo da Vinci, and Rembrandt that you can learn about through art and history.

- "Changing of the Guard" at Buckingham Palace: You can watch the famous ceremony outside of Buckingham Palace for free. It is a long-standing custom.

**Day 2: Adventures & Cultural Insights**

For those looking to enjoy London's outdoor areas and vibrant culture:

- Hyde Park & Kensington Gardens: These vast parks offer a peaceful retreat in the heart of London. Take a free walk around the Serpentine Lake, enjoy the Diana Memorial Fountain, or simply relax on the grass.

- Borough Market: Located near London Bridge, this market offers a sensory explosion of tastes and sights. While shopping might not always be budget-friendly, browsing the fresh produce, artisan goods, and street food is an experience in itself.

- Covent Garden: For a taste of London's street entertainment culture, head to Covent Garden. Watch free street acts ranging from magicians to musicians while soaking in the lively atmosphere.

**Day 3: Uncovering History & Traditions**

London's long past is filled with fascinating stories, and many historic sites are free to explore.

- The Tower of London: While the entrance fee to this historic fortress is not the cheapest, you can save money by exploring the nearby Tower Hill area, learning about the history of the British monarchy, and taking in the views of Tower Bridge.
- St. Paul's Cathedral: Admire the stunning building of St. Paul's from the outside. If you want to go

inside, keep an eye out for special offers or consider coming during free entry days.

**Day 4: Culinary Delights on a Budget**

London is a melting pot of cuisines, and you can enjoy great food without spending too much.

- Street Food: Try iconic British street food like fish and chips, or visit markets like Camden Market or Brick Lane for affordable and diverse options from around the world.
- Chinatown: A hidden gem for food lovers, Chinatown offers great deals on traditional Chinese dishes. It's a great place to grab lunch or dinner on a budget.
- Local Pubs: Many of London's pubs offer cheap meal deals, including traditional British fare like pies, sausages, and hearty stews. Look for "pub lunches" or daily deals to get the best value.

**Day 5: Off-the-Beaten-Path Experiences**

Explore some lesser-known parts of London that show the city's unique charm.

- Leadenhall Market: Explore this famous covered market, with its beautiful Victorian architecture. It's a great place to walk, window shop, or enjoy a coffee without spending much.
- Little Venice: Take a peaceful walk along the canals of Little Venice, a charming and quiet part of the city. You can even take a budget-friendly canal boat ride to Camden.
- Greenwich Park & The Royal Observatory: Greenwich Park gives sweeping views of the River Thames and the city skyline. While the Royal Observatory requires an entry fee, the park itself is free to tour, making it a great place for a relaxed afternoon.

**Final Tips**

London's public transportation system is fast, and you can save money by using an Oyster Card or Contactless payment for discounted fares on buses and the Tube. Look out for free events and festivals, especially in the summer months, as London often offers free outdoor concerts, theatre performances, and art exhibitions.

# CHAPTER 6

## Dining and Nightlife

London is a global melting pot of tastes and cultures, making it a haven for food lovers and night owls alike. Whether you're craving world-class fine dining, street food from every part of the globe, or a buzzing nightlife scene, London offers something for every palate and choice.

**Best Dining Experiences in London**

London's food scene is as varied as the city itself. From Michelin-starred restaurants to hidden gems in local neighborhoods, the city offers exceptional dining options that cater to every price.

Fine Dining:

For a unique gastronomic experience, head to The Ledbury in Notting Hill, a two-star Michelin restaurant known for its refined, seasonal British menu. Another top contender is Sketch, an artistic place offering avant-garde dining with a modern twist. Expect a sensory journey where every dish is as visually beautiful as it is delicious.

Casual Eats: If you're in the mood for something more laid-back but equally tasty, Dishoom is a must-visit. Serving up Mumbai-inspired dishes in a charming, vintage-style setting, this restaurant brings real Indian street food to the heart of London. Alternatively, Flat Iron is known for its unbeatable value—serving up quality steaks at a great price.

Street Food:

For a taste of London's lively street food scene, head to Borough Market for a wide variety of artisanal offerings. From freshly made pastries to gourmet sandwiches and foreign delicacies, this market has something for everyone. You can also explore Brick Lane for an array of curry houses and diverse foreign cuisines.

**Unique Dining Experiences**

Want to eat in a way that's as memorable as the food? London's dining scene includes a host of unique encounters.

- Dinner in the Sky: Enjoy a meal 100 feet above the ground with Dinner in the Sky. This thrilling eating experience offers a fine-dining menu while suspended in

the air, giving you panoramic views of the city skyline.
- The Shard: For unparalleled views of London while eating, head to Aqua Shard on the 31st floor of The Shard. The contemporary British cuisine here is complemented by stunning views that run for miles.
- Culinary Tours: Take a walking food tour through neighborhoods like Soho or Chinatown, where you'll try local favorites, street food, and regional specialties, all while learning about London's food culture.

**London's Vibrant Nightlife**

London's nightlife is famous, and whether you're after a trendy cocktail bar, a lively pub, or an all-night dance club, the city has it all.

Pubs & Traditional British Pints:

No visit to London is complete without tasting its pub culture. Whether it's a cozy corner pub or a lively place, British pubs offer a relaxed atmosphere to enjoy a pint of local ale. Head to The Churchill Arms in Notting Hill, a historic pub known for its stunning floral displays, or The Spaniards Inn in Hampstead for a pint in one of London's oldest drinking establishments.

Cocktail Bars:

For an elegant night out, explore London's high-end drink bars. The American Bar at The Savoy is one of the oldest and most famous cocktail bars in the world. For a more unique vibe, check out Dandelyan at the Mondrian Hotel, which focuses on creative and botanical-infused drinks.

Nightclubs & Live Music:

If you're in the mood to dance, head to Fabric, one of London's most famous nightclubs, known for its world-class electronic music scene. Alternatively, enjoy the city's live music scene at Ronnie Scott's Jazz Club in Soho, where legendary performers have graced the stage since the 1950s.

Late-Night Bites

For those who prefer to keep the night going, London offers plenty of late-night eating spots.

- Duck & Waffle: Located on the 40th floor of a building, this restaurant serves classic British dishes with a twist—perfect for a late-night bite while enjoying breathtaking views of the city.

- Vauxhall's Seven Dials Market: This busy food hall stays open late on weekends and offers everything from grilled cheese sandwiches to gourmet burgers and more.
- Chinatown: If you're craving late-night dim sum, Chinatown in the West End has numerous places open until the early hours of the morning.

**Trendy Neighborhoods for Dining and Nightlife**

Shoreditch: Known for its eclectic mix of trendy bars, food markets, and street art, Shoreditch is a hotspot for both eating and nightlife. Enjoy cutting-edge drinks at Nightjar, or head to Dishoom Shoreditch for some of the best Indian food in town.

Soho: This vibrant area offers everything from chic cocktail lounges to vibrant late-night eateries. It's also home to some of the best live music places in London, including Ronnie Scott's and The Borderline.

Covent Garden: Known for its street performers and restaurants, Covent Garden offers everything from elegant eateries to stylish wine bars. After dinner, explore the area's bars and theaters, with performances going well into the night.

From high-end dining to lively nightlife and quirky food experiences, London is a city that never stops when it comes to food and entertainment. Whether you're having a Michelin-star meal or sipping cocktails with a view, your dining and nightlife adventures in London will be unforgettable.

## Classic British Dishes and Where to Find Them

London's food scene is a melting pot of flavors, but no visit is complete without indulging in the city's iconic British dishes. From hearty pies to delicate afternoon teas, the capital is brimming with spots that serve up these typically British meals in style.

Fish and Chips

No dish is more synonymous with British cooking than fish and chips. Crispy, golden fish mixed with thick-cut fries make for a satisfying, classic meal.

- Poppies Fish & Chips (Spitalfields and Soho): One of London's best-known fish and chip shops, Poppies gives traditional, hand-cut chips and perfectly battered cod. The retro vibe adds to the experience, making it a must-visit for this popular dish.

- The Golden Hind (Marylebone): A long-standing tradition in Marylebone, The Golden Hind serves up some of the best fish and chips in the city. With its no-frills approach and generous servings, it's a favorite among locals and tourists alike.

**Sunday Roast**

The Sunday roast is a British tradition, often surrounded by roast meats, vegetables, Yorkshire puddings, and lashings of gravy. It's a meal meant to be enjoyed, especially when shared with friends or family.

- The Ledbury (Notting Hill): For a high-end version of the roast, head to The Ledbury, where a polished yet hearty Sunday roast is served in an elegant setting. Perfect for those wanting a fine dining experience with British comfort food.

**Full English Breakfast**

A hearty full English breakfast is the best way to start your day in London. Think eggs, bacon, sausages, baked beans, grilled tomatoes, mushrooms, and toast – all served with a hot cup of tea or coffee.

- The Breakfast Club (Soho and other locations): Known for its legendary full English, The Breakfast Club offers all the standard components served in generous portions. The relaxed, quirky vibe adds to the charm, making it a popular spot for early risers.

- Bill's (Various Locations): This chain offers a no-nonsense, satisfying breakfast that includes all the traditional ingredients. With its relaxed atmosphere, it's great for a leisurely start to your day.

**Steak and Kidney Pie**

For a comforting, savory meal, the steak and kidney pie is a traditional British treat. Tender beef and kidney encased in flaky pastry, this pie is a favorite of British bars.

- St. John Restaurant (Clerkenwell): Renowned for its focus on British ingredients, St. John offers a delicious and no-frills steak and kidney pie that displays the richness of traditional British flavors.

- St. Alban's (Pimlico): If you're looking for a classic, cozy bar experience, head to St. Alban's. Their steak and kidney pie is a standout, followed by rich gravy and creamy mashed potatoes.

**Bangers and Mash**

A comfort food favorite, bangers and mash consists of sausages served with creamy mashed potatoes, often accompanied by onion gravy.

- The Queen's Head (Belsize Park): This bar does bangers and mash perfectly, serving up high-quality sausages and mashed potatoes with a rich onion gravy that perfectly complements the dish.

- The Black Swan (Bow): A traditional East End pub where the bangers and mash are served with a generous helping of gravy, this local favorite is great for those in search of authentic British comfort food.

**Afternoon Tea**

No British trip is complete without a traditional afternoon tea. Indulge in delicate finger sandwiches, freshly baked scones with clotted cream and jam, and a range of teas.

- Claridge's (Mayfair): For a truly British afternoon tea, Claridge's offers one of the finest experiences in London.

Served in an opulent art deco setting, their selection of teas, sweets, and sandwiches is unmatched.

- The Ritz (Piccadilly): The Ritz is synonymous with luxury, and its afternoon tea is an iconic event. From the perfect scones to exquisite finger sandwiches, this classic tea service is a must for those who respect refined elegance.

**Sticky Toffee Pudding**

For dessert, sticky toffee pudding is a rich and indulgent pick. A moist sponge cake served with a warm toffee sauce and often topped with vanilla ice cream or custard, it's a real British treat.

- The Ivy (Covent Garden): For a sophisticated take on this British classic, The Ivy serves up a beautifully presented sticky toffee pudding, great for those looking for an upscale dessert experience.

- The Ledbury (Notting Hill): Another gem in Notting Hill, The Ledbury offers a delightful version of sticky toffee pudding, served with ice cream, giving a perfect sweet ending to a wonderful meal.

## Cheese and Biscuits

A classic British post-dinner dish, cheese and biscuits is often served as a savory snack after a rich meal, with a range of cheeses and crackers, sometimes accompanied by chutneys or fruit.

- Neal's Yard Dairy (Covent Garden): For an authentic cheese experience, head to Neal's Yard Dairy, where you'll find a curated range of British cheeses. Pair it with artisan crackers and a jar of chutney for a true taste of British custom.

- The Cheese Bar (Camden Market): A celebration of British cheeses, The Cheese Bar offers a range of artisanal cheeses and accompaniments, great for an after-dinner snack or a unique food experience

## Top Food Markets for Every Taste

London is a food lover's dream, and its bustling food markets are the heart of its diverse culinary scene. From global tastes to traditional British treats, these markets offer something for every palate. Here's a guide to the best food markets in the city, where you can enjoy fresh, locally grown ingredients, mouth-watering street food, and unique culinary experiences.

**Borough Market Best for: Classic British, International Street Food, Gourmet Ingredients**

One of London's oldest and most famous food markets, Borough Market is a must-visit for anyone wanting to explore a variety of cuisines. Located near London Bridge, it's a lively space where you'll find everything from fresh veggies to artisanal treats and street food.

- Must-Try Dishes: - Salt Beef Bagels: A London classic, **Borough Market's famous salt beef bagels are a great example of British comfort food.**

- Oysters & Seafood: Head to the seafood stalls for fresh oysters and other shellfish.

- Vegan Delights: For plant-based eaters, Borough offers a range of flavorful vegan dishes, like BBQ cauliflower tacos.

- Vibe: Traditional yet modern, with a mix of people and tourists.

**Camden Market Best for: International Cuisine, Alternative Vibes, Creative Food Stalls**

Camden Market is known for its eclectic, bohemian atmosphere and various food offerings. Whether you're looking for hearty meals or creative bites, this market has it all.

- Must-Try Dishes: - Arepas: Head to the Venezuelan food stalls for delicious arepas (cornmeal cakes filled with a range of toppings).

- Halloumi Fries: Crispy and indulgent, Camden's halloumi fries are a hit with both locals and tourists.
- Gourmet Doughnuts: For a sweet treat, don't miss the gourmet doughnuts from different stalls offering unique fillings.
- Vibe: Artsy, vibrant, and full of character, with street performers and live music adding to the mood.

**Spitalfields Market Best for: Trendy Bites, Artisan Foods, British and International Fusion**

Located in East London, Spitalfields Market blends past with modern tastes. It's the perfect place to discover artisanal goods, unique food stands, and specialty markets. Whether you're looking for brunch, lunch, or a snack, Spitalfields offers with flair.

- Must-Try Dishes: - Banh Mi: A Vietnamese sandwich filled with fresh veggies, herbs, and your choice of protein.

- Gourmet Grilled Cheese: A simple yet indulgent treat with rich toppings.

- Artisan Gelato: Spitalfields is home to some of London's best gelato stands, great for a refreshing treat.

- Vibe: Urban and trendy, with a bit of historical charm.

**Brick Lane Market Best for: Indian and Bangladeshi Flavors, Vintage Finds, Diverse Eats**

Famous for its curry houses and street food stalls, Brick Lane Market is a melting pot of tastes, especially from South Asia. On Sundays, the market is packed with food stalls, selling everything from spiced Indian delicacies to global snacks.

- Must-Try Dishes: - Curry: Whether you're after a traditional Bangladeshi curry or an Indian street-food twist, Brick Lane is the place to be for aromatic, delicious curries.

- Bagels: Don't miss the iconic Beigel Bake for a standard salt beef bagel or a sweet treat from the bakery.
- Fried Chicken: The fried chicken here is crispy, juicy, and served with a variety of interesting sauces.
- Vibe: Cultural, lively, and full of character, with street art and vintage shops lining the streets.

**Maltby Street Market Best for: Gourmet Delights, Hidden Gems, Artisanal Snacks**

A small yet vibrant food market located just south of Bermondsey, Maltby Street Market offers a selection of high-quality food that runs from fresh produce to indulgent treats. It's a hidden gem great for those in search of gourmet foods and unique flavors.

- Must-Try Dishes: - Artisan Cheese Toasties: For a warm and cheesy treat, try one of the artisan cheese toasties from the stalls.
- Fresh Pastries: From buttery croissants to rich Danish pastries, the market has plenty of fresh, indulgent baked goods.

- Craft Beers & Gourmet Coffee: Perfect for a mid-market pick-me-up, you'll find plenty of craft beer options and handmade coffee.

- Vibe: Cozy, laid-back, and a bit off-the-beaten-path, with a neighborhood feel.

**Southbank Centre Food Market Best for: Riverfront Views, Global Street Food, Quick Bites**

Located along the Thames, the Southbank Centre Food Market offers a variety of street food vendors serving quick, tasty dishes great for those on the go. Whether you're in the mood for global eats or British classics, this market has you covered, all while giving stunning views of the river.

- Must-Try Dishes: - Crispy Fish Tacos: Tasty, crunchy, and fresh, these tacos are a favorite at the Southbank market.

- Waffles & Pancakes: For a sweet treat, enjoy freshly made waffles or pancakes topped with rich toppings.

- Hot Dogs: Gourmet hot dogs, including international choices like bratwurst or spicy chorizo.

- Vibe: Relaxed and riverside, perfect for a casual, quick bite with a scenic background.

## Whitecross Street Market Best for: Street Food, Quick Lunches, Vegetarian-Friendly

Located near the city's financial area, Whitecross Street Market is perfect for busy workers and tourists alike. It's known for having a range of fast, fresh, and delicious street food with an emphasis on vegetarian-friendly options.

- Must-Try Dishes: - Vegetarian Buddha Bowls: Healthy, filling, and packed with flavor, the Buddha bowls here are a popular choice for vegetarians and vegans.

- BBQ Pulled Pork: Tender, spicy pulled pork served with fresh bread and tangy sauces.

- Falafel Wraps: A quick, tasty, and filling dish for those in the mood for something plant-based.

- Vibe: Fast-paced and vibrant, with a casual atmosphere great for a lunchtime break.

## Neighborhood-Specific Restaurant Recommendations

London is a city of culinary diversity, with each area offering its own unique dining scene. Whether you're in the mood for classic British fare, foreign cuisine, or cutting-edge gastronomy, there's a neighborhood in London that's sure to satisfy your cravings. Here's a roundup of top restaurant ideas in some of London's most popular areas for a memorable meal.

**Covent Garden Best for: Vibrant Atmosphere, European and Modern British Cuisine**

Known for its lively atmosphere and historic charm, Covent Garden offers a variety of dining choices perfect for a day of shopping and theater-going. This area is home to both traditional British pubs and innovative dining ideas.

- Dishoom (Indian): For a taste of Bombay in the heart of London, Dishoom is a must-visit. With its beautiful décor and mouth-watering Indian-inspired foods, it's an excellent spot for brunch, lunch, or dinner.

- The Ivy Market Grill (British): A local favorite, The Ivy Market Grill offers classic British meals with a modern twist, all served in a stylish, relaxed setting.

- Flat Iron (Steak): If you're in the mood for a great steak at a fair price, Flat Iron is the place to go. Known for its simple menu focusing on high-quality cuts of meat, it offers a truly memorable eating experience.

**Soho Best for: Trendy, Eclectic Dining, Global Flavors**
Soho is the beating heart of London's nightlife and food scene, packed with trendy places offering everything from classic cocktails to modern fusion cuisine. Whether you're after a quick bite or a leisurely dinner, Soho has it all.

- Hakkasan (Chinese): For upscale Cantonese food, Hakkasan is a Michelin-starred restaurant serving exquisite dim sum, roasted meats, and expertly crafted cocktails.

- Barrafina (Spanish Tapas): A bustling Spanish tapas spot, Barrafina offers a delightful array of small plates, from jamón ibérico to sizzling gambas, in a lively and social atmosphere.

- Palomar (Middle Eastern): For an Israeli-inspired feast, Palomar serves up rich, flavorful meals like sabich, polenta fries, and creamy hummus in a relaxed yet sophisticated environment.

**Shoreditch Best for: Hip, Indie Spots, Modern and Creative Cuisines**

Shoreditch is London's creative hub, with street art, live music, and a dining scene that fits its edgy vibe. The neighborhood is perfect for adventurous foodies looking out innovative and unique culinary experiences.

- Dishoom Shoreditch (Indian): Another location of the famous Dishoom, Shoreditch offers the same delicious Indian-inspired meals in a stunning setting that pays homage to Bombay's colonial architecture.
- Lyle's (Modern British): With its Michelin-starred chef and seasonal menu, Lyle's offers cutting-edge British food that emphasizes local ingredients and minimalist presentation.
- Pizza East (Italian): For pizza lovers, Pizza East serves

up wood-fired pies with fresh, quality toppings in a relaxed, industrial-style dining spot.

**Notting Hill Best for: Charming Cafés, Elegant Dining, and International Flavors**

Notting Hill is famous for its picturesque streets, boutique shops, and delightful dining spots. From casual cafés to upscale dining rooms, this area offers something for every mood and taste.

- The Ledbury (Modern European): A Michelin two-star restaurant, The Ledbury offers an unforgettable dining experience, with a menu featuring inventive modern European dishes and excellent service.

- Granger & Co. (Australian Café): Granger & Co. is the right spot for a relaxed brunch or lunch, offering light, healthy dishes with Australian-inspired flavors.

- Ottolenghi (Mediterranean): Known for its vibrant and seasonal Mediterranean recipes, Ottolenghi serves up fresh salads, pastries, and warm, aromatic dishes in a bright and airy space.

**Mayfair Best for: Fine Dining, Exclusive Spots, and International Flair**

Mayfair is home to some of London's most luxurious and elegant dining establishments, offering everything from fine French food to top-tier Japanese sushi. If you're looking for a high-end experience, this is the place to be.

- The Ledbury (Modern European): As one of the best restaurants in the world, The Ledbury offers exceptional modern European food with a focus on seasonal ingredients and stunning presentation.

- Nobu London (Japanese-Peruvian Fusion): Nobu is the go-to spot for upscale sushi, with creative dishes that blend Japanese techniques with Peruvian ingredients for a unique flavor experience.

- Sketch (Michelin-starred French): With its surreal décor and Michelin-starred menu, Sketch offers avant-garde French cooking, providing both an extraordinary meal and an unforgettable dining atmosphere.

## Camden Best for: Quirky Spots, Global Street Food, and Casual Vibes

Camden is a haven for alternative culture, and its food scene shows that. From laid-back eateries to global street food vendors, Camden is great for casual dining and a lively atmosphere.

- Moro (Spanish, Mediterranean): A favorite for tapas fans, Moro serves up a creative blend of Spanish and Mediterranean dishes, with a focus on fresh, seasonal ingredients.

- The Cheese Bar (Cheese-centric): If you're a cheese lover, The Cheese Bar offers a menu full of cheesy delights, from grilled cheese sandwiches to mac and cheese, all made with the best British cheeses.

- Koshari Street (Egyptian): For something a little different, Koshari Street serves up Egyptian comfort food, including koshari (a delicious mix of rice, beans, and chickpeas topped with fried onions).

**South Bank Best for: Riverside Dining, Relaxed and Scenic Spots**

The South Bank is great for a leisurely meal with beautiful views of the Thames. From iconic British fare to international dishes, there are plenty of choices along the river.

- Skylon (Modern British): With stunning views of the river, Skylon offers modern British cuisine with a refined twist, great for a special night out.

- Gillray's Steakhouse & Bar (Steakhouse): Located within the London Marriott Hotel, Gillray's offers a great selection of steaks, seafood, and cocktails, all with a view of the Thames.

- Swan, Shakespeare's Globe (British): For traditional British food with a view, Swan serves up British staples like fish and chips, shepherd's pie, and delicious desserts, all overlooking the river.

# CHAPTER 7

# Shopping and Souvenirs

London is a shopper's paradise, blending luxury names, unique boutiques, and quirky markets that offer something for every style and price. From iconic shopping areas to hidden gems, London offers memorable finds for fashion enthusiasts, antique hunters, and souvenir collectors alike. Here's your guide to the city's best shopping adventures.

**Oxford Street and Regent Street For: High-Street Fashion, Flagship Stores**

As the epicenter of London's retail scene, Oxford Street boasts over 300 shops featuring famous brands and flagship stores. Wander along the nearby Regent Street to find luxury brands and classic British shops like Liberty, known for its gorgeous Tudor-style architecture and high-end selection of clothing, accessories, and home goods.

- Key Stores: Selfridges, Zara, Nike, Liberty London
- Tip: Visit early in the day or mid-week to escape the busiest crowds.

**Covent Garden For: Boutique Shopping, Unique Finds**

Covent Garden is a lively area filled with eclectic shops, craft stalls, and charming markets, ideal for finding one-of-a-kind gifts. From quirky handmade crafts to British names like Mulberry and Charlotte Tilbury, it's a great spot to hunt for quality souvenirs.

- Highlights: Apple Market (crafts, antiques), Stanfords (world-famous map store), and Neal's Yard Remedies (natural skincare).
- Tip: Check out the street artists and enjoy a coffee at a nearby café as you shop.

**Knightsbridge and King's Road For: Luxury Shopping, Designer Labels**

Home to London's most famous luxury department shops, Knightsbridge is a must-visit for high-end shoppers. Harrods and Harvey Nichols offer everything from designer clothes to gourmet treats, while King's Road in nearby Chelsea has a mix of chic boutiques and fashionable home décor shops.

- Key Stores: Harrods, Harvey Nichols, Anthropologie, The Kooples.

- Tip: Don't miss Harrods' food hall for gourmet snacks and treats that make excellent presents.

## Camden Market For: Alternative Fashion, Vintage Finds

Camden Market is known for its vibrant atmosphere, alternative styles, and great street food scene. With hundreds of stalls offering everything from vintage clothing to handmade jewelry and quirky décor, Camden is a treasure trove for anyone looking to enjoy the city's eclectic spirit.

- Must-See Stalls: Cyberdog (futuristic fashion), Stables Market (antiques and collectibles), and The Vintage Collection.

- Tip: Go with an open mind and ready to haggle—vendors are often open to negotiation on prices.

**Portobello Road Market For: Antiques, Artisanal Goods**

Located in the heart of Notting Hill, Portobello Road Market is one of London's most famous street markets, especially for antiques and vintage treasures. It's a wonderful spot to find unique gifts, from antique watches to art prints, alongside fresh produce and food stalls.

- Key Finds: Antiques area on Saturdays, independent artists' stalls, secondhand books, and collectibles.
- Tip: Arrive early on weekends to get the best picks from antique dealers and escape the afternoon crowds.

**Spitalfields Market and Shoreditch Boutiques For: Independent Designers, Artisanal Gifts**

Spitalfields Market, located in the trendy East End, offers a mix of independent designers, vintage clothes, handmade crafts, and food vendors. Shoreditch, just around the corner, is dotted with cutting-edge boutiques and local designer shops, making it an ideal spot for anyone who enjoys London's creative edge.

- Highlights: The Sunday UpMarket (vintage and indie fashion), Boxpark (popup mall with small brands), and Brick Lane (vintage shops).

- Tip: Wander down Brick Lane for even more vintage finds and some of London's best street art.

**Greenwich Market For: Artisanal Crafts, Handmade Jewelry**

Nestled near the Thames, Greenwich Market is a charming spot offering artisanal crafts, handmade jewelry, and local artwork. Known for its bohemian vibe, it's a great place to pick up locally made items and handmade gifts you won't find anywhere else.

- Best Finds: Unique jewelry, art prints, and homemade candles.

- Tip: Stop by the nearby Cutty Sark for beautiful views and classic photo ops as you wrap up your shopping.

**Top London Souvenirs For: Timeless Mementos**

- Tea and Biscuits: Fortnum & Mason gives a beautifully packaged selection of English teas and luxury biscuits.

- British Chocolate: Brands like Cadbury and Charbonnel et Walker are well-loved for giving.

- London-Themed Memorabilia: From iconic red phone booth models to "Mind the Gap" gear, there's no lack of fun London-themed items in most gift shops.

- Union Jack Accessories: British fashion names like Ted Baker and Cath Kidston often have patriotic accessories.

## Famous Shopping Districts and What to Expect

London's shopping areas are world-renowned, offering everything from luxury labels and flagship stores to unique boutiques and artisanal markets. Here's a guide to some of the city's top shopping areas, each with its own unique vibe and offerings.

### Oxford Street: Iconic Retail Hub

Oxford Street is one of the most famous shopping streets globally, known for its high-street fashion stores and flagship names. With over 300 shops, it's a go-to location for fashion enthusiasts and trendsetters.

- What to Expect: Major shops like Zara, H&M, and Primark alongside high-end department stores like Selfridges.

- Shopping Tips: Visit mid-week or early in the morning to avoid crowds. The holiday season brings stunning lights and colorful window displays, making it an ideal time for a shopping spree.

**Regent Street and Jermyn Street:** British Elegance Just a short walk from Oxford Street, Regent Street and Jermyn Street offer an upscale experience with heritage names and luxurious boutiques.

- What to Expect: A mix of classic British labels like Burberry and Liberty, plus foreign luxury stores. Jermyn Street is known for its fine men's tailoring.

- Shopping Tips: Don't miss Liberty London, housed in a beautiful Tudor-style building, for a curated range of fashion, beauty, and home goods.

**Covent Garden:** Charming and Artistic Covent Garden is beloved for its lively atmosphere and eclectic mix of shops, artisan stalls, and unique eateries.

It's the right blend of high-end and bohemian shopping, with something for every taste.

- What to Expect: Quirky shops, handmade crafts, and British names like Mulberry. The Apple Market offers artisan crafts and antiques, while nearby Neal's Yard features natural beauty goods.

- Shopping Tips: Explore the outdoor plaza for street acts, and take a coffee break at a cozy café for people-watching in between shopping.

**Knightsbridge: Luxury and Glamour**
Knightsbridge is home to London's iconic luxury department stores, where designer fashion, gourmet treats, and exclusive beauty goods await.

- What to Expect: Harrods and Harvey Nichols are the stars here, giving high-end fashion, cosmetics, and home goods. The food halls at Harrods are famous for their exquisite selections of gourmet foods.

- Shopping Tips: Dress up a bit and enjoy the luxury! Check out Harrods' holiday sales for unique items, and make sure to visit the food hall for unique British delicacies.

**Camden Market: Alternative and Edgy**

Camden Market is where London's creative energy shines. Known for its alternative fashion, vintage finds, and lively food scene, this area is perfect for shoppers looking for something a bit more unique.

- What to Expect: Vintage clothing, handmade jewelry, and an array of food stalls offering world cuisines. Highlights include Cyberdog for futuristic fashion and the Stables Market for antique finds.

- Shopping Tips: Camden is busy on weekends, so visit early to get the best deals. Explore with an open mind—you're going to find something unexpected.

**Portobello Road Market: Vintage and Antiques Haven**

Located in picturesque Notting Hill, Portobello Road Market is best known for its amazing selection of antiques. It's a dream for vintage lovers and collectors looking for unique finds.

- What to Expect: A mix of antiques, secondhand books, retro clothes, and fresh food. The big market day is Saturday, when antique vendors line the street with treasures.

- Shopping Tips: Arrive early on weekends to browse antiques before the crowds. After shopping, explore Notting Hill's lively streets and cafés for a charming day out.

**Shoreditch and Spitalfields:** Indie and Artsy
East London's Shoreditch and Spitalfields areas are known for their artistic energy, trendy shops, and vintage markets. Here, you'll find independent designers and unique, handmade things.

- What to Expect: Spitalfields Market offers indie brands and artisan crafts, while Brick Lane is packed with vintage shops. The Boxpark pop-up mall is also close, featuring rotating shops and eateries.

- Shopping Tips: Sundays are ideal for Spitalfields and Brick Lane markets, where you can find everything from indie jewelry to vintage clothes. The street art here is amazing, so keep your camera ready.

**Greenwich Market:** Artisanal and Laid-Back
Greenwich Market is a lovely and slightly quieter

shopping spot where you'll find artisanal crafts, local artwork, and handmade jewelry.

- What to Expect: A mix of art prints, homemade crafts, and jewelry. It's especially popular with local artists and small business owners offering unique items.

- Shopping Tips: Take a stroll around the area to see the famous Cutty Sark and enjoy views along the Thames after shopping. Greenwich's slower pace makes it a relaxing choice to the bustling city center.

## Boutiques and Markets for Unique Finds

London's vibrant shopping scene goes beyond the famous department shops and high streets. For those wanting something special and off the beaten path, the city offers a wealth of boutiques and markets where you can discover unique, London-only treasures. Here are some of the best spots to find distinctive things, from handcrafted jewelry to quirky fashion and eclectic home decor.

### Spitalfields Market

Nestled in East London, Spitalfields Market combines history with a modern indie vibe, giving a mix of art, fashion, and handmade goods from local artisans.

- What to Expect: Independent designers, handmade jewelry, art prints, and vintage things. A rotating range of pop-up stalls means there's always something fresh and new.

- Insider Tip: Visit on weekends for the most complete selection, including unique finds like leather bags, upcycled clothing, and limited-edition artwork.

**Columbia Road Flower Market**

A feast for the senses, Columbia Road Flower Market is a haven for plant lovers and anyone looking for fresh blooms and garden-inspired house goods.

- What to Expect: Exotic flowers, succulents, and gardening tools, plus charming vintage shops and boutique stores lining the street.

- Insider Tip: Arrive early on Sundays to catch the best flower deals, then browse nearby antique and craft shops for unique home décor.

**Camden Passage, Islington**

Not to be confused with Camden Market, Camden Passage is a quaint pedestrian street packed with vintage shops, antique dealers, and unique boutiques.

- What to Expect: Vintage clothes, antiques, and an array of specialty shops selling everything from quirky gifts to one-of-a-kind furniture pieces.

- Insider Tip: Thursdays are the main market day for antiques, but shops are open all week for treasure hunts. Don't miss Annie's, a vintage boutique known for elegant, timeless pieces.

**Redchurch Street, Shoreditch**

Redchurch Street is known for its trendy boutiques, offering curated collections from contemporary British designers and exclusive foreign brands.

- What to Expect: High-end streetwear, minimalist home decor, and limited-edition art paintings. Boutique shops like Labour and Wait are praised for high-quality, stylish goods.

- Insider Tip: Explore nearby Brick Lane after shopping for street art and food stalls, making a full day of East London's creative scene.

**Portobello Road Market, Notting Hill**

Famous for antiques, Portobello Road Market also boasts vibrant areas with streetwear, vintage clothes, and artisanal goods.

- What to Expect: Antiques, vintage finds, and handmade jewelry. Unique things include retro clothing, rare vinyl records, and handmade trinkets.

- Insider Tip: Saturdays are best for antiques, while Fridays focus more on clothes. Look for the hidden shops tucked into side streets for the best-kept secrets.

**Greenwich Market**

Greenwich Market is a cozy spot to explore handmade crafts, boutique clothing, and art from independent makers.

- What to Expect: Handcrafted jewelry, local artwork, artisanal candles, and quirky gifts. This market is especially famous for small batch, one-of-a-kind items.

- Insider Tip: Check out the local artwork for sale—it's a cheap way to take home a piece of London's creative spirit. Then, relax with a snack from one of the fine food stalls.

## Liberty London

Though not a market, Liberty is a famous department store with a boutique feel, known for its distinctive Tudor architecture and curated collection of luxury items.

- What to Expect: Fashion, beauty items, home goods, and the famous Liberty fabrics, which make excellent souvenirs. Many things here are exclusive to Liberty.

- Insider Tip: Head to the home decor area for unique, design-forward pieces, and don't miss the selection of quintessentially British beauty and wellness products.

## Hackney Flea Market

A haven for vintage lovers, Hackney Flea Market brings together local vendors selling everything from retro clothes to handmade ceramics.

- What to Expect: Quirky home décor, retro clothes, and upcycled furniture. This market is beloved by London's hipsters and antique lovers alike.

- Insider Tip: Take your time to look through the stalls. The market often includes unusual finds like typewriters, old-school cameras, and artisanal pottery.

**Broadway Market**

A buzzing location for artisanal crafts, Broadway Market includes indie designers, handmade accessories, and food vendors.

- What to Expect: Unique gifts, independent fashion, and locally sourced foods. Broadway Market offers a lively atmosphere great for weekend browsing.

- Insider Tip: After shopping, relax at London Fields or explore the nearby cafes, many of which are beloved by locals for their specialty coffee and sweets.

London's markets and shops offer a refreshing break from typical souvenirs, making it easy to find something memorable. With each district representing its neighborhood's unique character, shopping here is as much about the experience as it is about the finds. Whether you're after old clothes, handmade jewelry, or distinctively British artwork, London has a shopping spot that fits your style.

## Souvenir Guide: Take Home a Piece of London

Bringing home a piece of London isn't just about picking up a memento—it's about capturing the spirit of the city in a way that feels personal and important. Here's a guide to authentic and memorable London souvenirs that go beyond the standard fridge magnets and keychains, giving you something unique to remember your visit by.

**Classic British Teas**

London is synonymous with tea culture, making fine tea an ideal, typically British souvenir.

- Where to Find It: Try Fortnum & Mason, Twinings, or Whittard of Chelsea for traditional blends, unique teas, and elegant gift sets. Each brand has a rich history and packaging that reflects classic British style.
- Top Picks: English Breakfast, Earl Grey, and London-themed tea mixes.

**British Chocolates and Sweets**

The UK is home to some world-famous chocolate brands, as well as smaller craft chocolatiers.

- Where to Find It: Try Harrods for luxury candies, or pop into any Marks & Spencer or Selfridges for classic British sweets like fudge, toffee, and chocolate.

- Top Picks: Look for Cadbury Dairy Milk bars, Thornton's toffees, and locally made fudge or salted caramel.

**Liberty Fabric and Accessories**

Known for its famous floral prints, Liberty London's fabrics are a beloved piece of British fashion history.

- Where to Find It: Head to Liberty on Regent Street for an entire floor dedicated to their famous prints, available in various forms, from scarves and ties to chair covers and fabrics.

- Top Picks: Liberty-print scarves or handkerchiefs make a stylish and easy-to-pack gift.

**Traditional British China**

Taking home British-made china can be a lasting keepsake, especially if you enjoy English tea customs.

- Where to Find It: Visit Wedgwood or Emma Bridgewater for beautifully made tea sets, mugs, and plates. Royal memorial mugs are also popular for those wanting a royal touch.

- Top Picks: Look for mugs, teapots, or small dishes with Union Jack or London landmarks for a traditional yet useful souvenir.

**Vintage Finds from London Markets**

London's markets are treasure troves of unique and vintage things that can't be found anywhere else.

- Where to Find It: Visit Portobello Road, Camden Passage, or Brick Lane for secondhand jewelry, old books, and unique decor items.

- Top Picks: Antique maps of London, vintage fashion accessories, and retro vinyl records make unique souvenirs.

**London Underground Memorabilia**

As one of the world's oldest and most famous transport systems, the London Underground offers its own line of gifts.

- Where to Find It: The London Transport Museum Shop has everything from replica posters and Tube map prints to socks and mugs adorned with the Underground's famous designs.

- Top Picks: Consider a classic Tube map picture, a vintage "Mind the Gap" sign, or a collectible Oyster card holder.

**Books from London Bookstores**

For book fans, a visit to London's famous bookstores offers not only a memorable experience but also a unique souvenir.

- Where to Find It: Daunt Books, Hatchards, and Foyles are among the best. Daunt Books, in particular, has travel-inspired versions that make excellent gifts.

- Top Picks: London-themed novels, guidebooks, or a classic British story by authors like Dickens or Austen.

**British Skincare and Beauty Products**

London has a thriving beauty business, with brands that stress quality ingredients and British heritage.

- Where to Find It: Visit stores like Lush, Neal's Yard Remedies, and Jo Malone for skincare products made with natural ingredients and British charm.

- Top Picks: Jo Malone fragrances, Neal's Yard skincare,

and Lush bath bombs offer a luxurious memory of your trip.

**Handmade Jewelry from Local Artisans**

For a truly personal piece, London's jewelry shops and markets offer handmade items that reflect the city's creative spirit.

- Where to Find It: Spitalfields Market, Columbia Road, and specialty boutiques in Shoreditch feature local designers making unique jewelry pieces.

- Top Picks: Look for rings, bracelets, or necklaces inspired by British themes or made with local materials.

**Royal Memorabilia**

With its rich royal past, London is the ideal place to pick up a bit of regal-inspired memorabilia, from subtle to statement pieces.

- Where to Find It: Shops near Buckingham Palace, Kensington Palace, and the Royal Collection Trust have high-quality things with official royal branding.
- Top Picks: Think commemorative coins, Union Jack flags, or copies of royal china and mugs.

**Savile Row Custom Accessories**

For something particularly unique, head to Savile Row, the heart of London's bespoke tailoring practice, for handcrafted accessories.

- Where to Find It: Boutique shops along Savile Row offer custom-made ties, cufflinks, and pocket squares for a taste of classic British craftsmanship.

- Top Picks: Opt for a silk tie, bowtie, or pocket square as a refined and stylish souvenir.

# CHAPTER 8

## Seasonal Events and Festivals

London is a city that celebrates every season in its own unique way, with festivals, markets, and events that offer locals and tourists something extraordinary throughout the year. From springtime blooms to winter events, here's what you can experience each season in London.

**Spring: Blooms and Open-Air Festivals**

As London wakes up from winter, spring brings gardens to life and outdoor events back to the city.

- Chelsea Flower Show (May): This world-famous flower show features elaborate gardens and innovative floral displays from top designers. Held at the Royal Hospital Chelsea, it's a must-see for garden lovers.

- Easter Celebrations: From Easter egg hunts at Kew Gardens to spring events in Hyde Park, the city offers family-friendly activities great for the season.

- Open Garden Squares Weekend: For one weekend in June, explore hidden gardens and private green spaces across London that are usually closed to the public.

**Summer: Culture and Carnival Vibes**

Summer in London is vibrant, with open-air events, music festivals, and outdoor dining on every block.

- Notting Hill Carnival (August): One of Europe's biggest street festivals, Notting Hill Carnival fills the streets with colorful costumes, Caribbean music, and an electric atmosphere over the August bank holiday weekend.

- Wimbledon Championships (June-July): Experience the excitement of the world's most prestigious tennis event. Visitors can queue for tickets or join locals in watching the matches on big screens across the city.

- British Summer Time (BST) Hyde Park: A music festival featuring top foreign artists in the scenic Hyde Park. Enjoy live acts under the summer sun or a starry sky.

**Autumn: Cultural Showcases and Seasonal Markets**

As the leaves turn, London's cultural scene comes alive, with film festivals, arts events, and cozy fall markets.

- London Film Festival (October): Attracting film buffs from around the world, this event showcases premieres, screenings, and Q&As with directors and actors, making it a highlight for cinema fans.

- Open House London (September): An architectural event where you can explore historic buildings, modern masterpieces, and hidden spaces usually closed to the public.

**Winter: Festive Lights and Holiday Cheer**

Winter turns London into a wonderland, with holiday markets, ice-skating rinks, and festive displays that capture the magic of the season.

- Winter Wonderland (November-January): Hyde Park's Winter Wonderland is a festive favorite, with holiday markets, exciting rides, an ice-skating rink, and food stalls. Perfect for families and friends alike.

- Christmas Lights and Window Displays: Oxford Street, Regent Street, and Covent Garden illuminate the city with beautiful holiday lights and decorated storefronts that draw in crowds from near and far.

- New Year's Eve Fireworks: London's Thames River fireworks display is iconic, giving a spectacular show to welcome the new year. Tickets are needed for viewing near the London Eye, but the show can be enjoyed from multiple vantage points across the city.

**Year-Round Events**

No matter the season, London's calendar is filled with events that offer something unique for every visitor.
- West End Shows: World-class theatre productions run all year, with classic plays, hit musicals, and exciting premieres that make the West End a must-visit for theatre fans.
- Changing of the Guard: Witness the traditional Changing of the Guard at Buckingham Palace, an iconic British event held throughout the year.
- Food and Drink Festivals: London's food scene is celebrated with events like the London Coffee Festival and London Cocktail Week, where visitors can try the best of local cuisine and creative beverages.

## Annual Events

London's annual events showcase the city's rich tradition, global impact, and vibrant cultural scene. These top events draw locals and visitors alike, each giving a unique way to experience London's spirit. Here's a guide to these can't-miss events, with tips on how to get the best out of each.

**Wimbledon Championships (June-July)**

As one of the most prestigious tennis events in the world, Wimbledon is a quintessential British experience. Enjoy strawberries and cream as you watch top players fight on the iconic grass courts.

- Make the Most of It: Tickets can be tough to come by, so try "The Queue" for same-day tickets or join fans in outdoor screenings across London, where you can soak up the excitement.

**Notting Hill Carnival (August)**

Europe's biggest street festival, Notting Hill Carnival is a vibrant celebration of Caribbean culture, complete with colorful costumes, steel bands, and mouth-watering street food.

- Make the Most of It: Get there early to beat the crowds, explore the main parade route, and check the schedule for shows. Plan your trip in advance, as public transport gets very busy.

**London Fashion Week (February & September)**

A hub for fashion lovers, London Fashion Week showcases cutting-edge British and foreign designers. Attend runway shows, pop-ups, and sample sales for a taste of high fashion.

- Make the Most of It: Tickets to big shows can be exclusive, but there are often events for the public. Keep an eye on the event's website for updates and consider exploring nearby shops for post-show shopping.

**Bonfire Night (November 5)**

Also known as Guy Fawkes Night, this event honors the failed Gunpowder Plot of 1605. Bonfires and firework shows light up the city in a festive tradition.

- Make the Most of It: Head to public parks like Alexandra Palace or Battersea Park for spectacular firework shows. Arrive early to find a good spot and bring a blanket and warm drinks for the evening.

**New Year's Eve Fireworks**

Ring in the New Year with London's famous fireworks display along the Thames, where crowds gather to watch a breathtaking show against the city's skyline.

- Make the Most of It: Tickets are needed for the main viewing areas, so book early. Alternative spots, like Primrose Hill or Parliament Hill, offer beautiful views without the crowd.

## What's Happening in 2025? Special Citywide Events

London is set to host a lineup of extraordinary events in 2025, giving visitors fresh experiences across culture, sports, art, and technology. Here's what's in store this year and why it's worth planning your trip around these unique events.

London Biennale of Contemporary Art 2025 marks the return of the prestigious London Biennale, a citywide show celebrating cutting-edge contemporary art from around the world. Expect immersive installations, provocative sculptures, and live performances in settings ranging from museums to outdoor spaces.

- What to Expect: Meet top international artists, participate in interactive workshops, and experience pop-up exhibits in unexpected places. Highlights will include large-scale works along the South Bank and at Tate Modern.

King's Coronation Anniversary Celebrations 2025 will also commemorate a major milestone in the reign of King Charles III, with citywide events celebrating his leadership and impact. Londoners and tourists alike can expect special exhibitions, royal parades, and more.

- What to Expect: Look out for the Royal Procession in The Mall, historical exhibitions at the Tower of London, and themed tours in key royal sites like Buckingham Palace and Windsor Castle.

**Tech Expo London:** Innovations in AI and Green Tech This year's Tech Expo will shine a spotlight on improvements in artificial intelligence and sustainability, gathering the world's top innovators in London's technology hub.

- What to Expect: Interactive AI shows, talks from industry leaders, and eco-friendly tech demos in Canary Wharf. This is a must-visit for tech enthusiasts eager to see the future in motion.

**150 Years of the London Underground: Celebration Events**

2025 marks the 150th anniversary of the London Underground, the world's longest metro system. To honor this historic milestone, special exhibits and guided tours will dig into the history of the Tube, its role in shaping London, and future plans.

- What to Expect: Special heritage trains, exclusive tours of closed stops, exhibitions at the London Transport Museum, and themed events in Tube stations. Get your hands on limited-edition souvenirs, including vintage-inspired Oyster cards.

Outdoor Cinema & Food Festival at Regent's Park
This year, London's beloved Regent's Park will change into a vibrant open-air cinema and food festival, featuring a rotation of great British films, international indie hits, and pop-up food stalls from London's top chefs.

- What to Expect: Bring a picnic blanket and relax with gourmet street food as you watch pictures under the stars. Enjoy diverse food choices, from traditional British fare to foreign delicacies, and catch screenings of iconic movies against the scenic park backdrop.

**Thames Light Festival**

In 2025, London will debut the Thames Light Festival, an awe-inspiring show of art and technology as the Thames River is illuminated with stunning light installations and projections by global artists.

- What to Expect: Walk along the riverbanks for breathtaking views, or book a river boat for an up-close experience. Look out for interactive displays and sustainable light technology, blending imagination with eco-friendly innovation.

From royal celebrations and milestone birthdays to world-class art and futuristic tech expos, London's 2025 calendar promises a year packed with unforgettable events. Whether you're here for art, history, tech, or simply a memorable city experience, 2025 offers a unique reason to explore London like never before.

## Monthly Event Highlights

Make the most of your London visit with this curated month-by-month guide to the city's top events in 2025. Whether you're interested in art, sports, or holiday festivities, London has something unique for every month.

**January** - New Year's Day Parade: Kick off the year with London's iconic New Year's Day Parade, featuring floats, marching bands, and performers from across the world.
- Winter Lights Festival at Canary Wharf: Wander through a dazzling display of light installations in Canary Wharf, featuring vibrant, interactive pieces by international artists.

**February** - Chinese New Year Celebrations: Head to Chinatown and Trafalgar Square for parades, dragon dances, and food stalls celebrating the Lunar New Year.
- Kew Gardens Orchid Festival: Visit Kew Gardens for its yearly orchid show, transforming the conservatories into a colorful paradise.

**March** - St. Patrick's Day Festival: Join the events in Trafalgar Square with live Irish music, dance, and traditional food.

- London Coffee Festival: Sample specialty brews and attend workshops at this coffee lover's dream event in Shoreditch.

**April** - London Marathon: Cheer on runners or join in the world-famous marathon that winds through London's scenic landmarks.

- Easter Egg Hunts and Events: Easter brings fun activities across the city, with egg hunts at sites like Hampton Court Palace and family-friendly events at the London Zoo.

**May** - Chelsea Flower Show: Admire stunning horticultural displays and garden designs at the prestigious RHS Chelsea Flower Show, a favorite among garden lovers.

- Museum Mile Festival: Enjoy late-night access, workshops, and tours in the Museum Mile's famous venues, including the British Museum and Charles Dickens Museum.

**June** - Trooping the Colour: Celebrate the King's birthday with this formal parade, featuring the Household Division and the Royal Family.

- Taste of London: Experience this food event in Regent's Park, offering tastings from London's best chefs, live cooking demos, and unique dishes.

**July** - Wimbledon Tennis Championships: Don't miss the excitement of the world's oldest tennis event. Get tickets or join a picnic with strawberries and cream nearby.

- Pride in London: Join one of Europe's biggest pride parades, celebrating diversity and inclusion with vibrant festivities across the city.

**August** - Notting Hill Carnival: Dance through the streets at Europe's biggest Caribbean event, known for its colorful costumes, music, and food stalls.

- Film4 Summer Screen at Somerset House: Enjoy outdoor movie nights at Somerset House, with classic and modern films on the big screen.

**September** - Open House London: Gain entry to iconic buildings usually closed to the public, from historic landmarks to contemporary architectural marvels.

- Totally Thames Festival: Celebrate London's river with art installations, live shows, and activities along the Thames.

**October** - BFI London Film Festival: Watch premieres of the year's best films, featuring global directors and stars, at cinemas across the city.

- Diwali on the Square: Experience Diwali celebrations in Trafalgar Square, complete with dance acts, food stalls, and fireworks.

**November** - Bonfire Night (Guy Fawkes Day): Join fireworks shows at spots like Alexandra Palace, celebrating the historic thwarting of the Gunpowder Plot.

- Christmas Lights Switch-On: See London change as holiday lights brighten up Oxford Street, Regent Street, and Covent Garden.

**December** - Winter Wonderland in Hyde Park: Soak in the holiday spirit with ice skating, Christmas markets, rides, and seasonal treats at Hyde Park.

- Christmas at Kew: Wander through illuminated paths and dazzling installations at Kew Gardens, a magical winter wonderland.

# CHAPTER 9

## Practical Tips and Travel Essentials

Get the most out of your London adventure with practical insights and important travel tips. From managing your money to staying safe, this chapter covers everything you need to travel like a seasoned Londoner.

1. Money Matters: Currency, ATMs, and Budgeting - Currency: The legal currency is the British Pound (£). Keep small bills and coins on hand, especially for small purchases and tips.

- ATMs & Credit Cards: ATMs are widely available, and most places accept major credit cards. For overseas travelers, cards with no foreign transaction fees can be a budget-friendly choice.

- Budgeting Tips: For an affordable London trip, opt for travel passes, check out free sites, and take advantage of local street food and markets for meals.

2. Staying Connected: SIM Cards and Wi-Fi - SIM Cards: Pick up a local SIM card at the airport or any cell shop for affordable data plans. Leading providers include

Vodafone, EE, and O2, with prepaid choices perfect for short-term visitors.

- Wi-Fi Access: Wi-Fi is easily available in cafes, museums, and even on public transport. Consider downloading offline maps and important apps for seamless connectivity on the go.

3. Health and Safety Tips - Emergency Services: Dial 999 for police, fire, or medical situations. Non-urgent medical assistance is offered at local clinics and hospitals.

- Traveler's Insurance: Comprehensive travel insurance can cover medical emergencies, cancellations, and theft, giving peace of mind during your visit.

- Staying Safe: London is usually safe, but standard precautions apply. Stay aware in busy areas, keep valuables close, and avoid secluded places at night.

4. Power Adaptors and Electronics - UK Power Sockets: The UK uses a Type G plug (three horizontal pins) with 230V. Bring a good adaptor and check your device's voltage compatibility.

- Charging on the Go: Portable chargers can be a lifesaver for keeping phones and gadgets powered through busy sightseeing days.

5. Weather-Ready Packing - Layers for All Seasons: London's weather can be unpredictable. Even in summer, pack a light jacket, umbrella, and layers for changing weather.

- Footwear: Comfortable walking shoes are a must. Consider waterproof options if you're coming during rainier months.

6. Language and Local Etiquette - Politeness: Londoners respect good manners—saying "please" and "thank you" goes a long way. Queueing (lining up) is important; always wait your turn.

- Mind the Gap: Familiarize yourself with popular phrases, such as "Mind the gap" in the Tube. It's not only useful but part of the local charm.

7. Sustainability Tips - Reduce Waste: Bring a reusable water bottle and shopping bag, as many shops charge for plastic bags.

- Eco-Friendly Dining: Support local cafes that value sustainability, and consider plant-based meals, which are widely available.

8. Apps and Tools for a Smoother Trip - Essential Apps: Download Citymapper for transport planning, the National Rail app for train schedules, and Google Maps for direction.

- Booking Tools: Many sites offer apps for online booking and wait-time updates, making it easy to secure tickets and skip the lines

## Budget-Friendly Tips for Exploring London

London doesn't have to break the bank. With some smart methods, you can enjoy the best of the city on a budget. Here's how:

1. Take Advantage of Free Attractions - Museums and Galleries: Many of London's world-class museums are free to enter, including the British Museum, Tate Modern, National Gallery, and Victoria and Albert Museum. Donations are appreciated but not needed.

- Parks and Gardens: Escape to green spaces like Hyde

Park, Regent's Park, and the famous Kew Gardens (which offers discounts and free entry on specific days).

2. Budget Transport Options - Oyster Card: Save on transportation with an Oyster Card or contactless payment, which caps daily journey costs and offers significant savings over paper tickets.

- Walk When You Can: London is highly walkable, with many sites close together, so take advantage of scenic walks instead of the Tube for short distances.

- Bike Rentals: Rent a Santander Cycle for just a few pounds and enjoy London's bike paths. Cycling can be both cheap and eco-friendly.

3. Affordable Eats - Street Food and Markets: London's street food scene is unbeatable. Try Borough Market, Camden Market, and Brick Lane for cheap, delicious bites from around the world.

- Supermarket Meals: Grab a meal deal from local supermarkets like Tesco, Sainsbury's, or M&S for a cheap lunch choice. Many grocery shops offer salads, sandwiches, and drinks bundled for a budget-friendly price.

- Happy Hours and Lunch Deals: Many clubs and restaurants offer discounted lunch menus and happy hour deals. Look for local spots in areas like Shoreditch and Soho.

4. Sightseeing on a Budget - Free Walking Tours: Many companies offer free walking tours with knowledgeable guides, allowing you to experience neighborhoods with a local's perspective. Just remember to tip your helper!

- Discounted Theatre Tickets: See a West End show without the high price tag by visiting the TKTS booth in Leicester Square or checking last-minute ticket apps for day-of savings.

- Viewpoints without the Price: Skip the high entry fees and head to free viewpoints like the Sky Garden or Greenwich Observatory for amazing views over London.

5. Smart Shopping for Souvenirs - Markets for Unique Finds: Head to local markets like Spitalfields for affordable, one-of-a-kind things instead of pricier tourist shops. Antique shops and weekend markets often have unique souvenirs at fair prices.

- Look for VAT Refunds: For non-EU visitors, claim back VAT on larger orders. This can be particularly useful if you're buying any high-ticket items.

## Cultural Etiquette: How to Blend In Like a Local

To make the most of your London visit, knowing the city's cultural norms will help you fit in and navigate social situations with ease. Here's how to fit in like a true Londoner:

1. Mind the Queue - Queuing is a way of life in London. Whether you're waiting for a bus, at a café, or entering a store, always stand in line and wait your turn. Jumping the queue is seen as rude and will likely get you some negative looks.

2. Use Polite Language - Londoners are known for their politeness. Phrases like "please," "thank you," and "sorry" are key to navigating talks. Saying "sorry" even when it's not your fault is part of the local politeness.

3. Avoid Overly Personal Questions - In London, personal privacy is important. Don't jump into questions about

someone's pay, family, or relationships unless you're well-acquainted. Stick to general topics like the weather, neighborhood events, or shared experiences.

4. Respect Public Transport Etiquette - On the Tube or buses, Londoners follow simple rules to ensure a smooth journey:

- Stand on the right side of stairs and allow others to pass on the left.
- Keep your talks low and avoid making phone calls.
- Let passengers leave before you board the train or bus.
- Be mindful of not blocking doors or seating places.

5. Tipping Customs - Tipping is popular but not compulsory in London. In places, a 10-15% tip is appreciated if service isn't included in the bill. For taxis, rounding up the fare is usual. For coffee or smaller services, a small tip or no tip is fine.

6. Respect the Local Drinking Culture - The British love their pub culture, and it's a key part of social life. When in a bar, it's polite to buy rounds of drinks for your group, but don't feel pressured to buy for everyone. Pubs close early, usually around 11 PM, so plan accordingly.

- If you're in a more formal setting, like a restaurant or bar, avoid excessive loudness and keep talks at a moderate level.

7. Dress Smart-Casual for Most Occasions - Londoners tend to dress smart-casual even in more relaxed settings. Whether you're going to dinner, a theater show, or just exploring the city, avoid overly casual clothing like flip-flops or athletic wear unless you're at a specific venue (like a gym or park).

8. Be On Time - Punctuality is important in London, especially for work meetings, social gatherings, and transport. Arriving on time is a sign of respect, whether you're meeting a friend for coffee or getting a train.

9. Embrace the Local Sense of Humor - The British are known for their dry humor and love of sarcasm. Don't take things too seriously—light-hearted teasing or irony is often used in talk. If in doubt, a smile or laugh will show you're in on the joke.

## Safety, Emergency Contacts, and Health Tips

Ensuring a safe and healthy trip to London will help you enjoy the city to the best. Here's a quick guide to keep you informed and prepared for anything during your stay.

1. Emergency Contacts - Emergency Numbers: - Police, Fire, Ambulance: Dial 999 (or 112) for all cases.

- Non-Emergency Police: Call 101 for non-urgent police issues.

- NHS (National Health Service) 111: For non-urgent medical help, dial 111. If you need a doctor, pharmacist, or dentist suggestion, this is your go-to number.

2. Safety Tips for Tourists - Stay Aware of Your Surroundings: While London is usually safe, be mindful of pickpockets, especially in crowded areas like markets, public transportation, and major tourist spots. Keep valuables in safe places, and avoid displaying expensive electronics or jewelry.

- Use Licensed Taxis and Rideshares: Stick to black cabs or licensed rideshare apps like Uber. Avoid taking rides from unmarked vehicles.

- Public Transport Safety: On the Tube or buses, keep your things close and avoid sleeping on the train. Late-night travel is usually safe, but be cautious in poorly lit areas.

- Nighttime Safety: Stick to well-lit areas when out at night and always use known routes to walk home or to your accommodation.

3. Health and Medical Tips - Travel Insurance: Always travel with complete health insurance that covers emergencies abroad. It'll give you peace of mind if you need to seek medical help.

- Medical Care: The UK has a great healthcare system, but non-residents may need to pay for services. If you're visiting for a short time, check with your insurance provider for medical coverage or consider purchasing travel insurance with healthcare benefits.

- Pharmacies: Pharmacies are easily found throughout London. Many provide over-the-counter medications for common ailments like colds, headaches, or digestive problems. Major chains include Boots and Superdrug.

- Prescriptions: If you need a specific prescription, make

sure to bring your doctor's note or consult a local pharmacy for help.

- Stay Hydrated and Protect from Sun: London's weather can be unexpected. Carry a reusable water bottle and apply sunscreen during summer months to protect yourself from the elements.

4. Staying Healthy During Your Visit - Food and Water: Tap water in London is safe to drink, and most places provide free water upon request. Street food is usually safe, but always ensure food is from reputable vendors.

- Avoid Overexertion: London is a place with lots of walking and exploring. To avoid tiredness or strain, wear comfortable shoes and take breaks between sightseeing. If you're exploring in hot weather, take frequent breaks and rest in shady places.

- Weather Preparation: London weather is often wet and can change quickly. Bring a umbrella and layer your clothes for warmth, as temperatures can drop unexpectedly.

5. Crime Prevention and Personal Safety - Keep Your Phone Secure: Use hotel safes or lockers to store valuables when visiting. Avoid using your phone in public places like busy streets or subways unless necessary.
- Trust Your Instincts: If something feels off, don't hesitate to remove yourself from the setting. Most Londoners are friendly, but it's always best to stay alert, especially in unfamiliar places.
- Street Safety: Some parts of London may be quieter late at night. Stick to more populated areas when walking after dark, and avoid short cuts through alleyways or badly lit streets.

Ensuring a safe and healthy trip to London will help you enjoy the city to the best. Here's a quick guide to keep you informed and prepared for anything during your stay.

1. Emergency Contacts - Emergency Numbers: - Police, Fire, Ambulance: Dial 999 (or 112) for all cases.
- Non-Emergency Police: Call 101 for non-urgent police issues.
- NHS (National Health Service) 111: For non-urgent

medical help, dial 111. If you need a doctor, pharmacist, or dentist suggestion, this is your go-to number.

2. Safety Tips for Tourists - Stay Aware of Your Surroundings: While London is usually safe, be mindful of pickpockets, especially in crowded areas like markets, public transportation, and major tourist spots. Keep valuables in safe places, and avoid displaying expensive electronics or jewelry.

- Use Licensed Taxis and Rideshares: Stick to black cabs or licensed rideshare apps like Uber. Avoid taking rides from unmarked vehicles.

- Public Transport Safety: On the Tube or buses, keep your things close and avoid sleeping on the train. Late-night travel is usually safe, but be cautious in poorly lit areas.

- Nighttime Safety: Stick to well-lit areas when out at night and always use known routes to walk home or to your accommodation.

3. Health and Medical Tips - Travel Insurance: Always travel with complete health insurance that covers

emergencies abroad. It'll give you peace of mind if you need to seek medical help.

- Medical Care: The UK has a great healthcare system, but non-residents may need to pay for services. If you're visiting for a short time, check with your insurance provider for medical coverage or consider purchasing travel insurance with healthcare benefits.

- Pharmacies: Pharmacies are easily found throughout London. Many provide over-the-counter medications for common ailments like colds, headaches, or digestive problems. Major chains include Boots and Superdrug.

- Prescriptions: If you need a specific prescription, make sure to bring your doctor's note or consult a local pharmacy for help.

- Stay Hydrated and Protect from Sun: London's weather can be unexpected. Carry a reusable water bottle and apply sunscreen during summer months to protect yourself from the elements.

4. Staying Healthy During Your Visit - Food and Water: Tap water in London is safe to drink, and most places provide free water upon request. Street food is usually

safe, but always ensure food is from reputable vendors.

- Avoid Overexertion: London is a place with lots of walking and exploring. To avoid tiredness or strain, wear comfortable shoes and take breaks between sightseeing. If you're exploring in hot weather, take frequent breaks and rest in shady places.

- Weather Preparation: London weather is often wet and can change quickly. Bring a umbrella and layer your clothes for warmth, as temperatures can drop unexpectedly.

5. Crime Prevention and Personal Safety - Keep Your Phone Secure: Use hotel safes or lockers to store valuables when visiting. Avoid using your phone in public places like busy streets or subways unless necessary.

- Trust Your Instincts: If something feels off, don't hesitate to remove yourself from the setting. Most Londoners are friendly, but it's always best to stay alert, especially in unfamiliar places.

- Street Safety: Some parts of London may be quieter late at night. Stick to more populated areas when walking after dark, and avoid short cuts through alleyways or badly lit streets.

## Packing Guide for Every Season

The weather in London isn't always reliable, so it's important to be ready for anything. Here's the best way to pack so you stay relaxed, stylish, and ready for anything, whether you're going in the summer, winter, or some other time of the year.

1. Spring (March to May): Layered Clothing Early in the morning and late at night, spring in London can be cool. In the afternoon, it can get warmer. Bring light sweaters or long-sleeved shirts, and for cold days, add a medium-weight jacket or coat on top.

- Good shoes for comfort: Many steps will need to be taken, so bring shoes that are both easy and waterproof for when it rains or shines.

• Umbrella: It often rains in the spring, so don't forget to bring a small umbrella to stay dry.

- Sunglasses: Sunglasses should always be handy for those rare bright days when the sun breaks through the clouds.

2. Summer (June to August) - Light and Breathable Clothing: London summers are usually mild, but when the sun's out, it can get warm. Pack T-shirts, shorts, light dresses, and linen pants to stay cool.

- Comfortable Footwear: Comfortable shoes are a must for walking tours or outdoor sports. Opt for sandals or sneakers that can handle a full day of exploration.

- Sunscreen and Hat: London might not always have powerful sunshine, but UV rays can still be strong, so pack sunscreen and a hat to protect your skin.

- Light Rain Jacket: Summer can bring unexpected showers, so a light rain jacket or packable poncho is important.

- Water Bottle: Stay hydrated while walking the city. Carry a reusable water bottle for refills throughout the day.

3. Autumn (September to November) - Warm Layers: Autumn brings cooler weather, so pack coats, sweaters, and long-sleeve shirts for layers. Opt for a woolen scarf or cardigan for extra warmth.

- strong Footwear: The weather can be unpredictable, so strong water-resistant shoes are a smart choice. Avoid open-toed shoes as it can get damp on wet days.
- Rain Protection: With higher chances of rain in the fall, bring a durable umbrella or a waterproof jacket.
- Warm Accessories: A knit hat, gloves, and a thermal layer can help keep you warm as temperatures dip in the evening.

4. Winter (December to February) - Heavy Coat: Winters in London are chilly but rarely freezing. Pack a warm winter coat that can keep out the cold. A down jacket or wool coat is a good pick.

- Thermal Layers: Layering is key in winter. Pack thermal tops, fleece-lined leggings, and woolen socks for extra warmth under your clothes.
- Sturdy Waterproof Boots: London streets can get slushy, so pack waterproof boots that are both stylish and useful.
- Accessories: A warm scarf, knitted hat, and gloves are important for staying cozy during outdoor activities.
- Umbrella: Even in winter, London gets frequent showers, so make sure to pack a sturdy umbrella for rain

protection.

5. General Essentials (Year-Round) - Power Adapter: London uses a Type G plug, so bring a universal adapter to charge your devices.

- Reusable Bag: Avoid single-use plastic with a foldable reusable bag to carry purchases or extras.

- Travel Guide/Map: While smartphones are handy, having a physical map or a guidebook can be helpful when exploring areas with bad signal.

**Packing Smart for London**

- Versatility is Key: London's weather can shift quickly, so pack clothes that can easily be layered or adapted for different circumstances. Stick to basic colors for easy mixing and matching.

- Weather-Ready Footwear: You'll walk a lot in London, so make sure your shoes are comfortable, flexible, and weather-appropriate.

# CHAPTER 10

## Day Trips and Excursions

While London has plenty to explore, some of England's most beautiful landscapes, historic sites, and charming villages are just a short journey away. Whether you're interested in picturesque countryside views, coastal retreats, or ancient castles, these day trips offer a fresh break from the city and showcase the diverse beauty of the nearby areas.

1. Windsor and Windsor Castle - Overview: Just an hour from London, Windsor is home to the iconic Windsor Castle, a favorite weekend house of British royalty. Wander the castle's grand rooms, and explore the scenic town with its riverside cafes and boutique shops.

- Highlights: State Apartments, Queen Mary's Dollhouse, St. George's Chapel

- Getting There: Direct train from London Paddington or Waterloo (around 1 hour)

2. Bath – Roman History and Georgian Splendor - Overview: Known for its Roman-built baths and Georgian

architecture, Bath is a UNESCO World Heritage city with a rich history and elegant charm. Perfect for those interested in history and architecture, a stroll through the cobblestone streets shows hidden gems and classic British beauty.

- Highlights: Roman Baths, Bath Abbey, Royal Crescent
- Getting There: Direct train from London Paddington (about 1.5 hours)

3. Oxford – The City of Dreaming Spires - Overview: Famous for its prestigious university, Oxford is a blend of historic charm and academic practice. Walk among centuries-old schools, soak in the scholarly atmosphere, and enjoy riverside punting or a visit to the university's museums.

- Highlights: Bodleian Library, Christ Church College, Ashmolean Museum
- Getting There: Train from London Paddington or Marylebone (about 1 hour)

4. Cambridge – A Riverside University City - Overview: Rivaling Oxford's academic history, Cambridge is known for its stunning architecture and serene river views. Enjoy

a guided punt along the River Cam, enjoy the Gothic architecture, and visit the world-famous King's College Chapel.

- Highlights: King's College Chapel, Fitzwilliam Museum, The Backs (riverside park)

- Getting There: Direct train from London Kings Cross or Liverpool Street (around 1 hour)

5. Brighton – Seaside Charm and Vibrant Culture - Overview: For a day by the sea, head to Brighton, a lively coastal town with a blend of traditional British seaside charm and modern artistic flair. Stroll along the pier, browse eclectic boutiques, and discover the Royal Pavilion's unique architecture.

- Highlights: Brighton Pier, The Lanes shopping area, Royal Pavilion

- Getting There: Direct train from London Victoria or London Bridge (about 1 hour)

6. The Cotswolds – Quintessential English Countryside - Overview: The Cotswolds, with its rolling hills and honey-colored stone towns, offers a taste of the idyllic English countryside. Take a tour of charming towns like

Bourton-on-the-Water and Stow-on-the-Wold, known for picturesque scenery, quaint shops, and cozy tea rooms.

- Highlights: Village walks, local markets, traditional tea houses - Getting There: Train from London Paddington to Moreton-in-Marsh (about 1.5 hours), then a short cab or bus ride

7. Canterbury – Medieval History and Gothic Beauty - Overview: Steeped in history, Canterbury is best known for its magnificent church, a UNESCO World Heritage site. Wander through medieval streets, visit historic sites, and soak up the atmosphere of one of England's most charming cities.

- Highlights: Canterbury Cathedral, Westgate Towers, St. Augustine's Abbey - Getting There: Direct train from London St. Pancras or London Victoria (about 1 hour)

8. Stonehenge and Salisbury - Overview: Discover the mystery of Stonehenge, one of the world's most famous prehistoric sites, followed by a visit to nearby Salisbury, home to a stunning cathedral and charming old town. Ideal for history fans and those curious about ancient Britain.

- Highlights: Stonehenge stone circle, Salisbury Cathedral, ancient town center - Getting There: Train from London Waterloo to Salisbury (around 1.5 hours), then a short bus or car to Stonehenge

9. Stratford-upon-Avon – Shakespeare's Birthplace - Overview: Literary fans can explore the home of William Shakespeare in this charming town. Tour Shakespeare's childhood house, visit the Royal Shakespeare Theatre, and wander the medieval streets of this scenic town.

- Highlights: Shakespeare's Birthplace, Anne Hathaway's Cottage, Royal Shakespeare Theatre

- Getting There: Train from London Marylebone to Stratford-upon-Avon (about 2 hours)

10. Leeds Castle and the Kent Countryside - Overview: Often referred to as "the loveliest castle in the world," Leeds Castle offers a stunning backdrop with lakeside views and sprawling grounds. Explore the ancient castle, get lost in the maze, and enjoy a day in the beautiful Kent countryside.

- Highlights: Castle tour, gardens, maze, falconry shows

- Getting There: Train from London Victoria to Bearsted, then a shuttle bus to the castle (about 1.5 hours)

**Tips for Enjoying Day Trips from London**

- Start Early: Catch an early train to maximize your time exploring each stop.

- Purchase Tickets in Advance: Many sites offer online discounts or timed tickets.

- Consider a Guided Tour: For hassle-free travel, guided day tours often include transportation, entry fees, and an expert guide, great for first-time visitors.

These day trips are an easy way to experience England's rich history, scenic landscapes, and charming villages—each just a short journey from the heart of London.

## Top Day Trips from London

London's prime location offers endless chances for quick escapes to historic towns, idyllic countryside, and coastal gems. Here are some of the most popular day trips, filled with travel tips for each destination.

1. Windsor and Windsor Castle - Why Visit: Home to Windsor Castle, the oldest and biggest occupied castle in

the world, this town offers a mix of regal charm and quaint riverside views.

- Highlights: Explore the castle, including St. George's Chapel and the State Apartments. Stroll through Windsor's cobblestone streets and waterfront parks.
- Getting There: Trains from London Paddington or Waterloo (about 1 hour).

2. Bath – Roman and Georgian Heritage - Why Visit: Known for its ancient Roman baths and elegant Georgian buildings, Bath is a UNESCO World Heritage city with a rich cultural past.

- Highlights: Tour the Roman Baths, Bath Abbey, and the Royal Crescent. Try the famous thermal waters at Thermae Bath Spa.
- Getting There: Direct trains from London Paddington (1.5 hours).

3. Oxford – The City of Dreaming Spires - Why Visit: Discover one of the world's oldest and most prestigious university cities, known for its stunning architecture and storied past.

- Highlights: Walk through Oxford's famous colleges, Bodleian Library, and Christ Church. Take a boat along the River Thames.

- Getting There: Trains from London Paddington or Marylebone (about 1 hour).

4. Cambridge – Riverside Beauty and Academic Legacy - Why Visit: Rivaling Oxford's scholarly history, Cambridge offers riverside views and iconic Gothic architecture.

- Highlights: King's College Chapel, the River Cam, and punting along the Backs.

- Getting There: Direct trains from London Kings Cross (around 1 hour).

5. Brighton – Seaside Vibes and Bohemian Charm - Why Visit: For a classic British seaside experience with lively arts and culture, Brighton is unbeatable.

- Highlights: Brighton Pier, the Royal Pavilion, and The Lanes shopping area.

- Getting There: Direct trains from London Victoria or London Bridge (about 1 hour).

6. Canterbury – A Walk Through Medieval England - Why Visit: Home to Canterbury Cathedral, this historic city is rich in medieval architecture and interesting history.
- Highlights: Canterbury Cathedral, St. Augustine's Abbey, and the city's small streets.
- Getting There: Trains from London St. Pancras or Victoria (about 1 hour).

7. The Cotswolds – Quintessential English Countryside - Why Visit: Known for its honey-hued towns and rolling landscapes, the Cotswolds offer a tranquil escape.
- Highlights: Explore quaint towns like Bourton-on-the-Water and Stow-on-the-Wold, known for tea rooms and boutique shops.
- Getting There: Trains from London Paddington to Moreton-in-Marsh (1.5 hours) followed by local bus or cab.

8. Stonehenge and Salisbury – Ancient Mysteries and Gothic Beauty - Why Visit: Witness the famous Stonehenge, a marvel of prehistoric engineering, and explore nearby Salisbury's historic charm.

- Highlights: Stonehenge, Salisbury Cathedral, and the lovely city center. - Getting There: Trains from London Waterloo to Salisbury (1.5 hours), with a short bus ride to Stonehenge.

9. Stratford-upon-Avon – The Birthplace of Shakespeare
- Why Visit: Perfect for literature enthusiasts, Stratford offers insights into the life and memory of William Shakespeare.
- Highlights: Shakespeare's Birthplace, Anne Hathaway's Cottage, and the Royal Shakespeare Theatre.
- Getting There: Trains from London Marylebone (about 2 hours).

10. Leeds Castle and the Kent Countryside - Why Visit: Often called "the loveliest castle in the world," Leeds Castle is surrounded by serene grounds and offers a day in the picturesque Kent countryside.
- Highlights: Explore the castle, maze, and falconry shows.
- Getting There: Trains from London Victoria to Bearsted, followed by a bus (about 1.5 hours).

**Quick Tips for Day Trippers**

- Start Early: An early train lets you make the most of your visit.
- Book Tickets in Advance: Save time and money by pre-purchasing tickets for popular sites.
- Consider Guided Tours: For stress-free travel, guided day trips include transportation and entry fees.

## How to Get to Windsor, Bath, the Cotswolds, and More

Exploring beyond London's city limits brings you face-to-face with the charm and history of England's countryside and famous towns. Here's how to reach some of the most popular day-trip destinations, along with must-see highlights for each area

1. Windsor - How to Get There: - Train: Take the train from London Paddington (transfer at Slough) or London Waterloo direct to Windsor & Eton Riverside stop. The trip takes about 1 hour.

- Coach: National Express buses also offer lines from central London to Windsor, taking around 1.5 hours.
- Highlights: - Windsor Castle: Tour the official home of

the British monarch, including St. George's Chapel and the State Apartments.

- The Long Walk: Enjoy scenic views with a leisurely walk from Windsor Castle through the beautiful Great Park.

- Windsor Great Park: Discover serene gardens, old oak trees, and landscaped grounds great for a picnic.

2. Bath - How to Get There: - Train: Direct trains from London Paddington take about 1.5 hours to Bath Spa station.

- Coach: National Express and Megabus trains from London take around 2.5 hours.

- Highlights: - Roman Baths: Wander through one of the best-preserved Roman bathhouses in Europe and experience 2,000 years of history.

- Bath Abbey: Visit this stunning piece of Gothic architecture with incredible stained glass windows and detailed stonework.

- Royal Crescent: Stroll along this famous row of Georgian townhouses for classic Bath architecture and views over the city.

3. The Cotswolds - How to Get There: - Train: Trains from London Paddington to Moreton-in-Marsh take about 1.5 hours. From here, you can explore nearby towns by bus or taxi.

- Car: Renting a car is ideal for exploring multiple villages in one day, giving you flexibility across the area.

- Highlights: - Bourton-on-the-Water: Often called the "Venice of the Cotswolds," this town offers picturesque stone bridges over the River Windrush.

- Stow-on-the-Wold: Known for its antique shops, tea rooms, and medieval charm, this hilltop town is truly English.

- Bibury: Don't miss Arlington Row, a row of quaint weavers' houses often regarded as one of the prettiest spots in England.

4. Oxford - How to Get There: - Train: Direct trains from London Paddington or London Marylebone to Oxford take about 1 hour.

- Coach: The Oxford Tube bus leaves frequently from central London and takes around 1.5 hours.

- Highlights: - Bodleian Library: Explore one of the oldest libraries in Europe, with an impressive collection and beautiful architecture.

- Christ Church College: A must-see for fans of history and architecture, and a famous site for Harry Potter fans.

- Ashmolean Museum: England's oldest public museum, offering art and archaeology collections covering thousands of years.

5. Brighton - How to Get There: - Train: Direct trains from London Victoria or London Bridge take about 1 hour to Brighton station.

- bus: National Express and other bus services take about 2 hours from central London.

- Highlights: - Brighton Pier: Experience classic beach amusements, food stalls, and beautiful ocean views.

- Royal Pavilion: This exotic, Indian-inspired palace with elaborate interiors is a must-visit for history fans.

- The Lanes: A maze of small streets filled with independent shops, boutiques, and cafés.

6. Stonehenge and Salisbury - How to Get There: - Train: Take a straight train from London Waterloo to Salisbury

(about 1.5 hours), then catch a bus or tour shuttle to Stonehenge.

- Tour: Many companies offer organized day tours from London that include transportation to Stonehenge and Salisbury.

- Highlights: - Stonehenge: Marvel at this prehistoric wonder, a lasting symbol of mystery and ancient engineering.

- Salisbury Cathedral: Home to the Magna Carta, this Gothic masterpiece boasts one of the tallest towers in the UK.

- Old Sarum: Explore the ruins of the old Salisbury settlement and enjoy sweeping views of the countryside.

7. Cambridge - How to Get There: - Train: Direct trains from London Kings Cross to Cambridge take about 1 hour.

- Coach: Coaches from central London take around 2 hours.

- Highlights: - King's College Chapel: Known for its incredible Gothic design and beautiful stained glass.

- Punting on the River Cam: Glide along the river, taking in the scenery and old college buildings.

- The Fitzwilliam Museum: Enjoy a rich collection of art and antiques from around the world.

## Themed Day Trips: Castles, Countryside, and Historic Towns

If you're looking to discover England's rich heritage and scenic landscapes beyond London, themed day trips offer an immersive way to delve into the country's history, culture, and natural beauty. Here's a guide to some of the best themed trips, whether you're drawn to grand castles, picturesque countryside, or storied towns that echo with tales of the past.

1. Castles and Royal Estates - Windsor Castle: Step into a thousand years of British monarchy at this royal palace, home to opulent State Apartments, St. George's Chapel, and the Changing of the Guard. Windsor's lovely town also offers quaint shops and riverside strolls.
- Leeds Castle: Located in Kent, this "loveliest castle in the world" is surrounded by a peaceful lake and gardens, complete with a maze, falconry shows, and seasonal events.
- Hever Castle: Once home to Anne Boleyn, this historic

castle in Kent offers beautifully landscaped grounds, water features, and a charming Tudor village atmosphere.

2. Countryside Escapes - The Cotswolds: Embark on a day of leisurely exploration through honey-colored villages like Bourton-on-the-Water and Stow-on-the-Wold, where boutique shops, tearooms, and historic buildings bring an idyllic charm.

- Surrey Hills: Just an hour from London, Surrey Hills offers rolling landscapes great for hiking and biking. Discover charming towns, scenic views, and local pubs nestled along country paths.

- Seven Sisters rocks: For breathtaking views of chalk rocks along the English Channel, visit the Seven Sisters. Enjoy seaside walks with panoramic ocean views and the peaceful beauty of the South Downs National Park.

3. Historic Towns and Cultural Experiences - Oxford: Famous for its elite university, Oxford offers a wealth of history and stunning architecture. Highlights include the Bodleian Library, Christ Church College, and guided walks that showcase literary landmarks.

- Stratford-upon-Avon: The birthplace of William Shakespeare, this medieval market town features sights like Shakespeare's Birthplace, Anne Hathaway's Cottage, and the Royal Shakespeare Theatre.

- Canterbury: This UNESCO World Heritage city is known for Canterbury Cathedral, a medieval beauty. Wander cobbled streets, visit the ruins of St. Augustine's Abbey, and experience the town's famous past.

4. Nature and Wildlife Adventures - Kew Gardens: Just outside London, the Royal Botanic Gardens at Kew offer vast landscapes filled with rare plants, historic glasshouses, and treetop walks.

- Whipsnade Zoo: One of the UK's largest wildlife parks, Whipsnade Zoo houses animals from across the globe in a spacious natural environment, great for families and nature lovers alike.

- New Forest National Park: Known for its wild ponies, this national park is a short journey from London and offers miles of trails, historic towns, and ancient woodlands.

# CHAPTER 11

## Sustainable Travel in London

London's commitment to sustainability makes it easier for travelers to experience the city while minimizing their environmental impact. By choosing eco-friendly choices, supporting local businesses, and embracing greener ways to explore, you can enjoy all that London offers while contributing to a positive environmental legacy. Here's how to make your London stay as sustainable as possible.

1. Eco-Friendly Transportation Options - Public Transit: London's extensive Tube, bus, and train network is efficient and eco-conscious. By using the city's public transportation, you lower your carbon footprint while traveling seamlessly across the city. Opt for an Oyster card or contactless payment for easy access to all transit choices.

- Bike Sharing: London's bike-sharing program, Santander Cycles, is a green way to get around while soaking in the sights. With docking stations across the city, cycling is a handy, affordable, and emission-free way to explore. Many areas also feature dedicated bike lanes for safe travel.

- Electric Taxis: For those times you need a car, look for London's growing fleet of electric black cabs. These low-emission vehicles are a cleaner option, helping to lower city pollution.

2. Sustainable Accommodation - Eco-Friendly Hotels: London offers a range of eco-certified hotels dedicated to sustainability. From reducing energy consumption to using local, organic products, these hotels emphasize green practices. Options include the One Aldwych and Treehouse London, both of which focus on eco-friendly design and low-impact operations.

- Green Apartment Rentals: Many apartment rental platforms feature eco-conscious listings that use sustainable materials and energy-efficient appliances, giving you the option to stay in a green place while feeling at home in London.

3. Dining with a Conscience - Farm-to-Table Restaurants: Embrace London's sustainable dining scene by visiting restaurants that stress seasonal, locally sourced

ingredients. Eateries like The River Café and Farmacy offer farm-to-table menus, showcasing organic produce and carefully sourced ingredients.

- Plant-Based Dining: London has a lively plant-based food scene, with countless vegan and vegetarian restaurants throughout the city. Places like Mildreds and The Gate highlight plant-based dishes that are as flavorful as they are eco-friendly.

- Zero-Waste Cafes: For a coffee break, try one of London's zero-waste cafes, such as The Fields Beneath, which focuses on minimizing waste with reusable containers, compostable packing, and a commitment to reducing food waste.

4. Shop Sustainably - Eco-Conscious Markets: London's markets, like Borough Market and Spitalfields, are filled with vendors selling local and organic goods. Buying from these markets supports small businesses and reduces the carbon footprint involved with long-distance shipping.

- Second-Hand and Vintage Shops: For unique finds, discover London's many vintage shops and second-hand boutiques, such as those in Shoreditch. By opting for pre-loved items, you lower demand for new production and support a circular economy.

5. Enjoy London's Green Spaces - City Parks and Gardens: London is home to an abundance of parks and gardens that not only offer a refreshing break from city life but also add to the city's biodiversity. Hyde Park, Kew Gardens, and Hampstead Heath are popular spots where tourists can enjoy nature responsibly. - Volunteer Activities: Some of London's parks and green spaces offer chances to volunteer. Whether it's helping with gardening, wildlife protection, or community events, volunteering is a rewarding way to give back to the environment while connecting with locals.

## Green Hotels, Restaurants, and Activities

London is full of eco-friendly options that make it easy for travelers to lower their carbon footprint. From sustainable hotels to plant-based restaurants and green activities, here are top tips for an environmentally conscious stay.

**Eco-Friendly Hotels**

- Treehouse London: This boutique hotel blends a playful atmosphere with sustainable practices. Its commitment to recycled materials, energy efficiency, and local sourcing makes it a top choice for eco-conscious tourists.

- The Zetter Hotel: Located in Clerkenwell, this hotel leads with green practices like clean energy sources and efficient water recycling. It's stylish and sustainably minded, with a cozy feel that makes it a London gem.

- One Aldwych: Known for its environmental efforts, this luxury hotel uses energy-saving systems, sustainably sourced materials, and eco-friendly products throughout. It's also located close to major sights, making it useful for green travel.

**Green Dining Spots**

- Farmacy: Located in Notting Hill, this plant-based restaurant is passionate about sustainability. It offers a creative, organic menu made from local ingredients, with zero single-use plastics and a dedication to composting food waste.

- The Gate: This family-run vegetarian restaurant has sites in Marylebone, Islington, and Hammersmith, each offering vibrant dishes made with fresh, seasonal ingredients. The Gate's eco-friendly method includes sustainable sourcing and recycling practices.

- The Fields Beneath: For a coffee break, this zero-waste cafe in Kentish Town is a must. They're entirely vegan and value minimal waste, offering compostable packaging and encouraging customers to bring reusable containers.

**Sustainable Activities**

- Cycling with Santander Cycles: London's bike-sharing system offers a clean, fast way to explore the city. With thousands of docking stations, it's easy to pick up and drop off bikes as you explore eco-friendly routes through London's neighborhoods and parks.

- Thames River Walks: Enjoy scenic riverside views and find iconic landmarks on foot along the Thames Path. Walking is not only eco-friendly but also offers a unique perspective on the city.

- Volunteer Conservation Days: Connect with local groups, like London Wildlife Trust, and get involved in preserving the city's green spaces. Whether it's tree planting, wildlife monitoring, or helping with park maintenance, it's a satisfying way to give back to nature during your visit.

**Eco-Conscious Shopping**

- Borough Market: This historic market supports local farmers and vendors with organic produce, sustainable goods, and seasonal ingredients. It's a great spot for environmentally friendly shopping and tasting local flavors.

- Second-Hand Finds in Shoreditch: The vintage stores and thrift shops in Shoreditch provide unique, pre-loved clothing and items that are as sustainable as they are stylish, allowing you to shop without adding to fast fashion.

## Eco-Friendly Itineraries and Transportation Options

Explore London sustainably with thoughtful itineraries and eco-conscious travel choices. From scenic walking routes to bike-friendly paths, you can enjoy the city while minimizing your environmental footprint.

**Green Itinerary Highlights**

- Historic Walking Tour Begin your day with a walking tour of historic sites like Westminster Abbey, Big Ben, and Buckingham Palace. Walking allows you to soak in the sights, enjoy the city's beauty, and avoid traffic emissions.

- Green Spaces and Parks Spend your afternoon visiting Hyde Park, Regent's Park, or Hampstead Heath. These lush green areas provide a peaceful escape and allow you to experience London's natural beauty, all while supporting the city's commitment to green public spaces.

- Eco-Conscious Museum Visits Many of London's top museums, like the Tate Modern and the Natural History Museum, adopt sustainable practices. Spend a few hours indoors enjoying art and history while supporting institutions that value sustainability.

- Sustainable Dining Spots Wrap up the day with a meal at one of London's eco-friendly restaurants, like Farmacy or The Gate, where menus feature plant-based and organic dishes found locally.

## Green Transportation Options

- Santander Cycles London's public bike-sharing system, Santander Cycles, offers an easy and cheap way to get around. With thousands of docking stations, you can hop on and off bikes throughout the city, avoiding emissions and traffic while getting a more intimate view of London's neighborhoods.

- Public Transit with an Oyster Card For longer routes, use the London Underground, buses, or overground trains with an Oyster Card or contactless payment. These choices are far more eco-friendly than driving and are among the most efficient ways to travel through the city.

- Electric Black Cabs When you need a car, consider London's famous black cabs, many of which are now electric. These low-emission taxis provide a sustainable option for private rides, with drivers who know the city well and can help you reach your destination efficiently.

- Thames Clipper

For a scenic and green option, try the Thames Clipper, an eco-conscious river bus that connects key points along the Thames. The Clipper runs on hybrid engines, reducing emissions and offering a relaxing, unique view of London from the wate

## Reducing Your Environmental Footprint

Enjoy London carefully by incorporating these sustainable practices into your trip. From mindful dining to waste reduction, here are easy yet impactful ways to minimize your environmental footprint while making the most of your visit.

### Sustainable Choices for Dining and Shopping

- Choose Local and Organic Foods Opt for restaurants that stress local, seasonal, and organic ingredients. London offers a variety of farm-to-table and plant-based dining choices, like Mildreds and Farmacy, that reduce food miles and support sustainable farming practices.

- Bring Reusable Items

Pack a reusable water bottle, utensils, and shopping bag to decrease single-use plastics. Many of London's sights, like museums and galleries, have water refill stations, making it easy to stay hydrated without creating waste.

- Eco-Conscious Shopping

Look for London-based designers or shops that offer sustainable brands. Neighborhood markets, such as Borough Market or Spitalfields, often support local artists and offer unique, eco-friendly souvenirs.

## Waste Reduction and Responsible Tourism - Practice the 'Leave No Trace' Principle

Whether you're exploring city parks or historical sites, avoid littering and respect the space. Carry out all waste, and if recycling is available, take advantage of it to keep the world clean for others.

- Opt for Low-Waste Accommodations Many of London's hotels have adopted low-waste and energy-efficient practices. Choose places with a commitment to sustainability—some even offer in-room recycling and biodegradable toiletries.

**Low-Impact Transportation**

- Walk or Cycle Whenever Possible Walking and biking are the most healthy ways to explore London. Not only will you lower emissions, but you'll also experience the city's neighborhoods up close. Rent a bike from Santander Cycles or join a guided walking tour to find hidden gems without leaving a footprint.

- Use Public Transport Wisely Public transit is one of the best ways to get around. Opt for the Tube, buses, or Thames Clippers for longer routes, and avoid taking taxis or rideshares unless necessary.

**Support Eco-Friendly Experiences - Visit Eco-Conscious Attractions**

Some attractions, like Kew Gardens and the London Wetland Centre, are dedicated to conservation and environmental teaching. By visiting these sites, you'll help initiatives that protect wildlife and promote sustainability.

- Choose Sustainable Tours Seek out tours that fit with eco-friendly values, such as walking tours or small group excursions led by locals. These types of tours reduce crowding and limit environmental impact, while giving an authentic experience.

# CHAPTER 12

## Planning Tools and Resources

Maximize the ease and enjoyment of your London trip with a selection of essential tools and resources. From apps to travel websites, these tips will help you plan, navigate, and explore the city like a seasoned traveler.

Must-Have Travel Apps

- City mapper A comprehensive app that simplifies managing London's vast transportation network. City mapper offers real-time directions for buses, trains, and the Tube, with options for walking and biking routes as well. Essential for avoiding delays and keeping on track.

- Google Maps Your go-to for mapping routes, finding nearby places, and even identifying landmarks. Download offline maps for added ease, so you're never lost even without internet access.

- Visit London App

This official app by Visit London offers a treasure trove of information on sites, events, and activities across the city. It's packed with exclusive deals and insights, perfect for those wanting insider tips and timely updates.

Online Planning Websites - Time Out London
Get the latest info on events, restaurant openings, and neighborhood guides with Time Out London. Known for its in-the-know recommendations, it's a great resource to discover unique experiences and avoid tourist traps.

- Transport for London (TfL)

The official TfL website is essential for transport updates, fare calculators, and route planners. Check it for Tube schedules, ticket information, and tips on avoiding peak travel times.

- London Pass and Other Attraction Passes

Websites like the London Pass give you access to discounted multi-attraction tickets. Explore different pass options to save on important sites like the Tower of London, Westminster Abbey, and more, making it a convenient choice for budget-conscious travelers.

**Resources for Cultural Insights and Language - Culture Trip**

Culture Trip offers rich articles and guides on local customs, food, and traditions. Perfect for tourists wanting to dive into London's unique cultural tapestry and get tips on how to blend in with the locals.

- Duolingo or Google Translate

While English is spoken widely, a language app can still come in handy for specific scenarios. Brush up on British phrases and pronunciations or use Google Translate for instant help with any language needs.

**Packing and Weather Tools**

- Weather Pro or AccuWeather

Check the forecast with accuracy before each day's journey. London's weather can be uncertain, so having a reliable weather app on hand ensures you're always dressed for the conditions.

- Pack Point

A smart packing app that makes tailored packing lists based on your trip duration, activities, and forecasted weather. This app saves time and ensures you're prepared, rain or shine.

**Budgeting and Money Management Tools**

- XE Currency Converter

Keep track of currency changes with XE Currency. It's perfect for knowing exactly what you're spending, especially when visiting multiple shops or eating out.

- Split wise

If you're traveling with friends or family, Splitwise helps keep shared costs organized. Track group costs with ease and settle up without the stress of managing receipts.

# High-Resolution City and Neighborhood Maps

Ensure you're never lost in London by accessing high-resolution maps that provide a clear, detailed view of the city and its varied neighborhoods. Whether you're exploring the historic alleys of Westminster, the trendy streets of Shoreditch, or the open spaces of Hyde Park, these resources keep your trip smooth and straightforward.

Best Sources for High-Quality Maps

- Google Maps

Offers detailed, interactive maps with features for navigation, neighborhood attractions, and live traffic reports. Download individual London neighborhoods offline for easy access without data.

- City mapper

Known for its precise, user-friendly maps tailored to major cities, City mapper provides public transport details, real-time updates, and multiple route choices, making it a favorite among locals and tourists alike.

- Transport for London (TfL) Maps

TfL's official website gives free, high-quality maps of the London Underground, bus routes, and overground train lines. It's an important resource for anyone using public transportation.

- Visit London Official Maps

Visit London's website offers downloadable PDFs and interactive maps, covering both major sites and lesser-known areas. This includes specific neighborhood guides with marked landmarks, eateries, and scenic places.

- Streetwise London Maps

For tourists who prefer hard copies, Streetwise offers laminated, durable maps sold online or at bookstores. Their detailed city and neighborhood maps are easy to carry, giving quick reference points for landmarks and public transport stops.

## Essential Apps and Websites for Easy Navigation

Navigating London is a breeze when you have the right tools at your hands. From real-time transport updates to insider tips on the best local spots, these important apps and websites are your go-to resources for a seamless and enjoyable journey through the city.

1. City mapper - What it does: Offers the most efficient lines for buses, trains, tubes, and even walking. It offers step-by-step instructions, live updates, and alternatives for any journey.

- Why use it: City mapper simplifies transportation in London, showing real-time updates and the fastest ways to get to your destination—ideal for both visitors and locals.

- Available on: iOS, Android.

2. Google Maps - What it does: Provides detailed directions for driving, walking, biking, and using public transportation. You can watch routes, track real-time traffic, and discover nearby attractions.

- Why use it: It's a versatile, widely trusted app that works worldwide, perfect for tourists who need reliable mapping and live traffic data.

- Available on: iOS, Android.

3. Transport for London (TfL) App - What it does: The official app for London's transport system, it gives live updates on the Tube, buses, trams, trains, and river services. It also includes fare information and maps.

- Why use it: It's the most reliable source for all London public transport-related queries, with up-to-the-minute info.

- Available on: iOS, Android.

4. Uber - What it does: A well-known ride-hailing service that offers fast, reliable transportation across London,

especially if you're looking to avoid the crowded Tube or buses.

- Why use it: It's great for those who need a private ride or want to avoid the complexities of public transport.
- Available on: iOS, Android.

5. Visit London Website - What it does: The official tourist website offers detailed guides on attractions, events, neighborhoods, and secret gems. It's a one-stop shop for everything you need to plan your stay.
- Why use it: It's constantly updated with new information, events, and travel tips, helping you stay on top of everything happening in London.
- Available on: Website (www.visitlondon.com).

6. Time Out London - What it does: Features a curated list of the best things to do, eat, and see in London, along with reviews, event information, and insider guides to the city.
- Why use it: Time Out is ideal for finding the best activities, from popular attractions to hidden gems that locals love.
- Available on: Website (www.timeout.com/london), iOS, Android.

7. The London Pass App - What it does: Helps you plan your trip by giving access to major attractions with a single pass, offering exclusive discounts and skipping the line options.

- Why use it: If you plan on visiting several attractions, the London Pass gives you a stress-free experience, plus the app offers helpful guides on how to make the most of your pass.

- Available on: iOS, Android.

## Local Language Tips and Common British Phrases

Understanding the local lingo is a fun and engaging way to connect with Londoners. While English is the main language, British slang and expressions can add flavor to your conversations. Here are some useful language tips and popular British phrases that will make you sound like a local.

1. "Cheers!" - What it means: Used as a lighthearted way of saying "thank you" or "goodbye." It's also the usual toast when having a drink.

- How to use it:

- "Thanks for the help!" — "Cheers!"

- "Cheers, mate!" — "Goodbye, friend!"

- "Cheers!" — A toast before drinking.

2. "Fancy a cuppa?" - What it means: "Would you like a cup of tea?" Tea is a beloved British tradition, and giving someone a "cuppa" is a sign of hospitality.

- How to use it:

- "It's a bit chilly outside, fancy a cuppa?"

- "We're having tea, would you like one?"

3. "Brolly" - What it means: An umbrella.

- How to use it:

- "It's starting to rain, better grab your brolly!"

- "Do you have a spare brolly?"

4. "I'm knackered!" - What it means: "I'm really tired."

- How to use it:

- "I've been walking all day, I'm absolutely knackered!"

- "It's been a long week, I'm knackered."

5. "Mate" - What it means: A term for a friend or buddy, often used lightly.

- How to use it:

- "Alright, mate?" (Hello, friend)

- "I'll catch up with you later, mate."

- "Cheers, mate, I appreciate it!"

6. "All right?" - What it means: A nice way to ask "How are you?" or "Are you OK?"

- How to use it:

- "All right, mate?" (Hey, how's it going?)

- "You look a bit down, all right?

7. "Bugger off!" - What it means: A stronger way of saying "go away," but it can be playful or harsh, based on context.

- How to use it:

- "Oh, bugger off! I'm busy!" (Dismissive)

- "Bugger off, I'm trying to relax." (Friendly fun)

8. "Proper" - What it means: It means "real" or "serious" and is often used to stress something.

- How to use it:

- "That was a proper good meal!" (It was a really great meal!)

- "He's a proper football fan." (A dedicated sports fan)

9. "In a minute" or "In a sec" - What it means: It means "in a little while" or "soon," but it doesn't always refer to exactly one minute.

- How to use it:

- "I'll be with you in a minute." (I'll be there soon.)

- "Just a sec, I'll grab my coat."

10. "Taking the mick" - What it means: To mock or tease someone in a fun way.

- How to use it:

- "Stop taking the mick out of me!"

- "I can't believe you're taking the mick with that story."

**Language Tips:**

- Politeness is key: Londoners respect good manners. Phrases like "please," "thank you," and "sorry" go a long way.

- "Sorry" is versatile: In the UK, "sorry" is used even for minor inconveniences, like bumping into someone on the street or interrupting a talk.

- Formality is common: British people tend to be more formal with strangers. Use "sir" and "madam" in more formal settings, but "mate" is great for casual interactions.

# CHAPTER 13

## Insider Tips and FAQs

Planning a trip to London can be thrilling, but it often comes with its own set of questions and unknowns. To help you make the most of your visit, we've compiled a list of insider tips and answers to commonly asked questions. Whether you're a first-time visitor or returning for another adventure, this chapter will provide useful insights to ensure you have a seamless and unforgettable experience in the UK capital.

Insider Tips for a Stress-Free Visit

1. Buy an Oyster Card or Contactless Travel Card

London's public transportation system is one of the best in the world, but it can be expensive without the right card. The Oyster Card is a prepaid smart card that gives discounted fares on the Tube, buses, and even the Thames Clippers river bus. Alternatively, using a contactless bank or credit card works just as well. This is the most cost-effective and easy way to get around.

2. Avoid Peak Hours on the Tube

The London Underground can get incredibly busy, especially during rush hours (around 8–9 AM and 5–6 PM). If you can, try to plan your sightseeing and travel outside these busy periods. Not only will this make your trip more comfortable, but you'll also experience a more relaxed atmosphere on public transport.

3. Walk as Much as Possible

While London's public transport is great, walking is one of the best ways to explore the city. Many of the most iconic sites, like Buckingham Palace, Trafalgar Square, and Westminster Abbey, are within walking distance of each other. A stroll along the Thames also offers beautiful views of the city's skyline and historic bridges.

4. Use Free Museums and Attractions

London is home to many world-class museums and galleries that are completely free to visit. The British Museum, the National Gallery, the Tate Modern, and the Natural History Museum are just a few examples. Take advantage of these free sites to enrich your trip without breaking the bank.

5. Check the Weather Before You Go

London weather can be unexpected, with rain at any time of year. Always take a small, portable umbrella or a raincoat, especially if you plan to explore the city outdoors. Layering clothes is also a good idea, as temperatures can change quickly throughout the day.

6. Take Advantage of London's Parks and Gardens

When it comes to finding a quiet place to unwind, London offers an abundance of beautiful green spots. Whether it's the vast open spaces of Hyde Park or the serene settings of Kew Gardens, take time to escape the hustle and bustle of city life by enjoying one of London's many parks or gardens.

7. Book Tickets in Advance for Popular Attractions

London is a city that draws millions of visitors every year, and its most popular attractions can often be booked up. To avoid long queues or missing out, it's always best to buy tickets for popular sights like the London Eye, the Tower of London, and West End theatre shows well in advance.

**Frequently Asked Questions (FAQs)**

1. What's the best time to visit London?

London is a year-round destination, but the ideal time to visit relies on your preferences. The summer months (June to August) offer warm weather and outdoor events but are also the busiest and most expensive. For fewer crowds and milder weather, spring (April to June) and autumn (September to October) are great choices. Winter (December to February) can be cold and rainy, but it also brings lively holiday markets and fewer tourists.

2. How do I tip in London?

Tipping in London is welcomed but not obligatory. In restaurants, a tip of 10–15% is typical if service is not included in the bill. For taxis, rounding up to the nearest pound or giving 10% is usual. It's always nice to leave a small tip if you receive exceptional service.

3. Is it safe to walk around London at night?

London is generally a safe city, but like any big metropolis, it's important to stay alert, especially after dark. Stick to well-lit areas, avoid isolated streets, and use your best judgment. Popular nightlife areas like Soho and Shoreditch are usually bustling late into the night, but always plan your route and be aware of your surroundings.

4. What should I wear when visiting London?

London is a fashion-forward city, but comfort is key. Be prepared for varied weather, so layering your clothes is important. A waterproof jacket, comfortable walking shoes, and an umbrella are suggested. If you plan to dine in upscale restaurants, dress smart-casual—no need for a full suit unless stated.

5. How do I get from Heathrow Airport to Central London?

There are several transportation routes from Heathrow Airport to the city:

- Heathrow Express: The quickest option, going just 15–20 minutes to Paddington Station.

- London Underground (Piccadilly Line): A more affordable choice, though it takes around 45 minutes to an hour.

- Taxi: Taxis are available outside the terminals, though this is the most expensive choice, especially during rush hour.

- Shuttle Bus: Several bus services are offered for budget-friendly transport.

6. Are there any free walking trips in London?
Yes! Several companies offer free walking tours where you can tip the guide at the end if you liked the tour. These tours cover a range of themes from history walks around the City of London to street art tours in East London.

7. What should I do if I lose something in London?
If you lose something in a public place, you can call the Lost Property Office of Transport for London (TFL) or the venue where you lost the item. You can also check with the nearby police station, though in most cases, lost items in public transport are handed over to TFL's lost and found department.

## FAQs: What Every Visitor Wants to Know

When it comes to making a trip to London, visitors often have a lot of questions. Whether it's about getting around, the best places to eat, or safety concerns, this part answers the most common questions to help you prepare for an unforgettable stay in the UK capital.

1. What's the best way to get around London?

London boasts one of the most efficient public transportation networks in the world, so getting around is easy and handy. Here are the top ways to travel the city:

- Oyster Card or Contactless Payments: The most cost-effective way to travel on public transport (buses, the Tube, trams, and trains) is by using an Oyster card or mobile payment card. Both offer large savings compared to buying paper tickets.

- The Tube: London's underground system is the quickest way to travel between big attractions. It's reliable, fast, and links almost all parts of the city.

- Buses: London's iconic red buses are not only useful but also a great way to see the city. They run 24/7, and some paths even offer panoramic views.

- Walking and Cycling: Many of London's top sights are within walking distance of each other. You can also take a bicycle through the Santander Cycles bike-sharing program, which allows you to explore at your own pace.

2. How do I get from Heathrow Airport to central London?

There are several transportation routes from Heathrow to the city center:

- Heathrow Express: This is the fastest and most direct way to central London, taking just 15–20 minutes to reach Paddington Station. It runs every 15 minutes.

- London Underground (Piccadilly Line): For a more budget-friendly choice, take the Piccadilly Line on the London Underground, which takes approximately 45 minutes to get to central London.

- Taxi: While cabs are available outside the airport, they can be pricey, especially during peak hours. Expect a journey of about 40–60 minutes based on traffic.

- Shuttle or Coach Services: Several shuttle and coach services operate between Heathrow and central London, offering an affordable alternative to taxis.

3. What are the must-see sites in London?

London is packed with iconic buildings and world-class museums. Some of the top sights you won't want to miss include:

- The British Museum: Home to over eight million works of art and artifacts, including the Rosetta Stone and Egyptian mummies.

- The Tower of London: A must-visit for history buffs, this 1,000-year-old fortress houses the Crown Jewels.

- Buckingham Palace: Witness the Changing of the Guard at the official home of the British monarch.

- The London Eye: This giant viewing wheel offers breathtaking views of the city skyline.

- Westminster Abbey and the Houses of Parliament: Iconic sites of British politics and history.

4. What's the best time to visit London?

London is a year-round destination, but the best time to visit varies on what you want to experience:

- Spring (April to June): Temperatures are mild, and the city is filled with blooming flowers in places like Hyde Park and Kew Gardens.

- Summer (July to August): This is the most popular time to visit due to warmer weather and numerous outdoor events. However, it can also be busy and more expensive.

- Autumn (September to November): The weather stays

pleasant, but the crowds thin out, making it an ideal time to explore.

- Winter (December to February): London's winter charm shines through with holiday markets, ice skating rinks, and Christmas lights, though temperatures can be chilly.

5. Is London an expensive place to visit?

London can be expensive, but there are ways to enjoy the city on a budget:

- Accommodation: While luxury hotels can be pricey, London offers a wide range of affordable accommodations, including hostels, small hotels, and budget-friendly chains. Consider living outside of the city center for lower prices.

- Food: You don't need to spend a lot on food. Street markets like Borough Market or Camden Market offer delicious, cheap meals. Casual eateries, like pub lunches, are also great choices.

- Free sites: Many of London's top sites are free, including the British Museum, the National Gallery, and Hyde Park.

- Discount Passes: Consider purchasing a London Pass or

similar city passes that give entry to multiple attractions at a discounted price.

6. Are there any safety worries for visitors in London?

London is usually a very safe city, but like any major metropolis, it's important to stay aware of your surroundings:

- Pickpocketing: As with any busy city, keep an eye on your belongings, especially in crowded places like Oxford Street or on the Tube.

- Stay in well-lit areas: If you're out late at night, try to stay in well-lit, populated places. Avoid walking alone in less busy areas after dark.

- Emergency Services: The emergency number in the UK is 999, which can be dialed for police, fire, or medical situations.

7. How do I use the Tube and buses?

- The Tube: The London Underground works on a zone-based system. Simply tap in and out using your Oyster card or contactless payment card at the start and end of your trip. Make sure you know which line and way you need to take before boarding.

- Buses: The best way to use the bus is by tapping your Oyster card or contactless payment card when you board. Unlike the Tube, there is no need to check out when you get off the bus.

8. Can I drink alcohol in public places?

In London, it's usually acceptable to drink alcohol in public areas such as parks or by the Thames. However, be aware of local rules and regulations:

- Pubs and Restaurants: Alcohol is widely available in London's pubs, restaurants, and bars.

- Public Transport: It's illegal to drink alcohol on public transportation such as the Tube, buses, or trains, with a few exceptions on certain train lines.

- Parks: While it's legal to drink in most public parks, be respectful of the space and mindful of local laws, especially in more tourist-heavy areas.

9. What's the tipping etiquette in London?

Tipping in London is appreciated but not required. Here's a general guide:

- Restaurants: A service charge of 12.5% is often included in your bill. If not, a tip of 10-15% is normal if service is good.

- Taxis: It's usual to round up the fare or tip around 10%.

- Bars and Pubs: Tipping is not required, but it's a kind gesture to leave small change.

10. What are some common British words to know?

Understanding a few British phrases can make your trip more enjoyable:

- "Cheers!" – A lighthearted way of saying thank you.

- "Fancy a cuppa?" – Would you like a cup of tea?

- "I'm knackered." – I'm very tired.

- "Mind the gap." – A warning on the Tube platform to be careful of the room between the train and the platform.

## Insider Secrets for Avoiding Crowds and Finding Hidden Gems

London is one of the world's most visited cities, and while there's no lack of iconic landmarks, the crowds can often be overwhelming. But fear not – with a few insider tips, you can sidestep the tourist traps, discover lesser-known gems, and enjoy a more relaxed, authentic experience of the city. Here's how to navigate London like a local and find its hidden treasures.

## 1. Explore Hidden Parks and Green Spaces

London is known for its beautifully manicured parks, but the biggest ones, like Hyde Park and Regent's Park, often draw large crowds, especially on sunny days. Instead, seek out the city's quieter, lesser-known green spaces:

- Hampstead Heath: This vast and varied park offers stunning panoramic views of the city from Parliament Hill, as well as tranquil woods, ponds, and meadows, making it a perfect escape from the hustle and bustle.
- Epping Forest: Just a short trip outside the city, Epping Forest is a sprawling nature reserve with peaceful trails, old woodlands, and wildlife. It's ideal for those looking to enjoy nature without leaving London completely.
- Postman's Park: Tucked away near St. Paul's Cathedral, this small, serene park features a touching memorial to heroic self-sacrifice, where you can pause and think in a peaceful setting.

## 2. Skip the Crowded Markets and Visit Quieter Ones

While markets like Borough Market and Camden Market are world-famous, they're also consistently busy. For a more relaxed shopping experience, check out these lesser-known markets:

- Spitalfields Market: Located in the East End, Spitalfields offers a mix of vintage clothing, independent art, and unique food stalls, all in a lively but less chaotic atmosphere.

- Maltby Street Market: A smaller, more intimate food market found in Bermondsey, Maltby Street serves up mouthwatering artisanal treats without the overwhelming crowds.

- Columbia Road Flower Market: On Sundays, this market is a bloom of color with an array of fresh flowers and plants. It's busy but still keeps a charming, local vibe that makes for an excellent photo op and peaceful stroll.

3. Discover Lesser-Known Museums and Galleries

While the British Museum and the National Gallery are definitely must-sees, they can also be crowded with tourists. For a quieter but equally enriching experience, try these hidden cultural spots:

- The Sir John Soane's Museum: This quirky, former home of the famous architect Sir John Soane is filled with art, antiques, and curiosities. It's an off-the-beaten-path gem that offers a fascinating look into history and architecture.

- The Wellcome Collection: A great trove of exhibits exploring the intersection of medicine, science, and art, this free museum near Euston is rarely crowded and offers something for everyone, from interactive exhibits to thought-provoking installations.

- The Hunterian Museum: Located in the Royal College of Surgeons, this museum is a fascinating collection of medical oddities, surgical tools, and anatomical models, all tucked away from the main tourist routes.

4. Take the Scenic but Less-Visited Routes

London has an extensive network of canals and hidden waterways that are great for exploring without the usual crowds. Rather than fighting your way through the city's busiest streets, try these beautiful routes:

- Regent's Canal: For a quiet walk or bike ride, head to Regent's Canal. Starting from Little Venice, you can follow the canal's tranquil path through Camden, King's Cross, and beyond, passing by lovely houseboats and peaceful green spaces along the way.

- South Bank's Riverside Walks: While the South Bank is popular, there are plenty of quieter riverside paths, especially around the lesser-known areas near the National Theatre and Gabriel's Wharf. These spots offer great views of the Thames and access to independent shops and cafes.

5. Dine Off the Beaten Path

London is a foodie haven, but to avoid the crowds, venture into some of the city's lesser-known neighborhoods where you can taste local flavors without waiting in long lines:

- Chinatown (Soho): While Chinatown itself can be busy, exploring the hidden gems around Gerrard Street, such as smaller noodle shops or family-run restaurants, can give you an authentic taste of Chinese food away from the tourist crowds.

- Exmouth Market: Tucked away in Clerkenwell, this street is full of independent places offering everything from fresh street food to trendy cafes, perfect for a relaxed lunch.

- Brick Lane: While Brick Lane is famous for its curry houses, don't miss some of the quieter spots that specialize in unique dishes from Bangladesh, India, and the Middle East, giving a more intimate dining experience.

6. Take a Scenic Ride on a Lesser-Known Boat

Most visitors know about the Thames Clippers and the iconic boat tours that take you past sites like the Tower of London and the London Eye. But if you want a more peaceful experience, try these alternatives:

- Thames Traditional Boating Company: Explore the river on a traditional wooden boat for a more intimate and relaxed experience, full with historic charm.

- Kew Gardens Boat Ride: For something a bit different, the boat ride around Kew Gardens offers a quiet way to enjoy the sights while being surrounded by nature.

7. Visit Hidden Streets and Quirky Neighborhoods

London's charm lies in its eclectic mix of old and new, and the city is full of little-known streets and neighborhoods just ready to be explored:

- Neal's Yard: A colorful, hidden courtyard in Covent Garden filled with independent shops, restaurants, and yoga classes. It's a peaceful escape from the crowds and a great spot for a photo.

- Leadenhall Market: Known for its beautiful Victorian architecture, Leadenhall Market is a shopping arcade that's often ignored by tourists. It's less crowded than nearby sites like Borough Market, and its historic vibe makes it a great spot for a leisurely wander.

- Greenwich's Historic Streets: While Greenwich is famous for the Observatory and Maritime Museum, there are also charming historic streets like the charming old pubs and odd shops near the Cutty Sark.

8. Visit London's Secret Gardens

While the famous Kew Gardens draws crowds, there are other secret gardens spread around London where you can enjoy tranquility and stunning green spaces:

- The Sky Garden: An indoor garden with panoramic views of the city, the Sky Garden is a hidden gem found at the top of the "Walkie-Talkie" building. It's free to enter, but booking in advance is important.

- The Roof Gardens: Located in Kensington, The Roof grounds offer a beautiful and unexpected green space atop a building, where you can relax among landscaped grounds and even spot flamingos.

**Final Thoughts**

London is full of secrets waiting to be revealed. By going off the beaten path, you can enjoy a more relaxed, authentic experience away from the crowds. Whether you're seeking quiet green places, hidden cultural gems, or unique dining experiences, there's always something new to discover in this vibrant city. Follow these insider tips and you'll not only escape the crowds, but also get a true taste of what makes London so unique.

## "London Like a Local": Tips to Experience the City Authentically

London is a dynamic city, teeming with history, culture, and hidden gems that often go unnoticed by the average visitor. While the must-see landmarks are iconic, there's something especially special about experiencing London through the eyes of a local. If you're looking to truly enjoy the city's authentic charm, follow these tips to make the most of your time in London and experience it like a true Londoner.

1. Embrace the Pub Culture

Pubs are the heart of British social life, and no trip to London is complete without experiencing this famous part of its culture. Skip the overly touristy spots around major sites and head to local favorites where Londoners unwind after work or on the weekend.

- The Churchill Arms in Kensington is a hidden gem, known for its lush floral exterior and cozy atmosphere, serving a great selection of beers and classic pub fare.
- The Dove in Hammersmith is a historic riverside pub, tucked away from the crowds, offering spectacular views over the Thames and a true local vibe.
- Join a Pub Quiz: A staple of pub culture, pub quizzes are a fun way to connect with locals. Check out the listings for the best weekly quizzes going in neighborhoods like Islington or Shoreditch.

2. Take the Tube During Off-Peak Hours

While the London Underground is an easy way to get around, it's also one of the busiest public transport systems in the world. To experience the Tube like a Londoner, avoid the rush hour crush and try to travel either early in the morning or after 9:30 a.m. when the crowds thin out.

- Pro Tip: Get a Oyster Card for cheaper fares or use mobile payment methods like a credit or debit card to avoid long lines at ticket machines. Avoid tourist hotspots like Oxford Circus or Leicester Square during peak times to enjoy a more relaxed trip.

3. Explore Neighborhoods Beyond the Tourist Spots

While Westminster, Covent Garden, and the West End are certainly beautiful, Londoners cherish their local neighborhoods, where you'll find the true essence of the city's diversity and charm.

- East London's Shoreditch offers trendy art galleries, independent cafes, and street art, giving you a taste of the city's cutting-edge creativity. It's a great place to wander, soak in the energy, and find hidden treasures.

- Notting Hill might be known for the film, but it's also a peaceful neighborhood to stroll, with charming boutiques, independent shops, and the famous Portobello Road Market. It's a spot loved by locals for its quiet charm.
- Hackney is another center for young Londoners. From vibrant nightlife to vintage shops and hidden cafes, this area perfectly embodies the city's spirit of innovation and coolness.

4. Savor Local Food at Markets and Street Stalls

London's food scene is as different as its people. While you can always indulge in classic fish and chips or an afternoon tea, Londoners know that the real culinary gems can be found at the city's street markets and local food stands.

- Borough Market is a must-visit for food lovers, but if you're looking for a less crowded option, head to Maltby Street Market in Bermondsey for some of the best artisanal food and delicious street snacks.
- Brick Lane is another hidden gem, with its long-running reputation for great curry houses. Try a bagel with salt beef or grab a falafel from one of the sellers – it's the local way to snack on the go.

- Food trucks are a quintessential part of the London street food scene. From tacos in Camden to gourmet burgers in Shoreditch, these mobile places offer tasty bites that locals swear by.

5. Spend Time in the Parks and Green Spaces

While tourists come to Hyde Park and Regent's Park, Londoners have their own peaceful refuges where they unwind and escape the urban buzz. The city's vast network of parks offers plenty of room to relax, exercise, or enjoy nature without the crowds.

- Hampstead Heath gives panoramic views of London and a genuine escape into nature. Enjoy a quiet walk through its wooded areas, or take a dip in the outdoor swimming ponds (weather allowing).

- Clapham Common is a favorite for picnics, jogs, and Sunday strolls. Locals love to meet up with friends or take their dogs for a walk here.

- Greenwich Park is one of the city's oldest and most scenic parks, giving views of the River Thames and access to the Royal Observatory, but without the throngs of tourists.

## 6. Catch a Local Theatre Show

London is home to world-renowned theatres, but for a truly local experience, explore off-West End shows or visit fringe theatres where up-and-coming talent performs. The local theatre scene offers cutting-edge, intimate shows that showcase London's artistic diversity.

- The Old Red Lion Theatre in Islington is a local favorite, offering a mix of comedy, drama, and thought-provoking shows.

- The Bush Theatre in Shepherd's Bush is another secret gem, hosting cutting-edge plays and plays about modern London life that speak to the city's multicultural character.

- The Vaults in Waterloo offers experimental performances in a quirky, underground setting, giving an immersive experience unlike anything you'll find in the West End.

## 7. Get Involved in London's Cultural Festivals

London's year-round festival calendar offers plenty of opportunities to experience the city's vibrant local culture. Many events celebrate the variety and creativity that

Londoners hold dear, so get involved with one of these lesser-known cultural celebrations.

- The Thames Festival celebrates the river's historic and cultural significance, having boat races, live music, and street food along the banks.

- London's International Theatre Festival brings together the best of local and international talent, showing innovative and groundbreaking performances across various venues in the city.

- Camden Fringe Festival is another alternative to the bigger Edinburgh Fringe, giving a platform for up-and-coming artists, with comedy, theatre, and experimental performances.

## 8. Chat with Locals and Discover Hidden Spots

Londoners are friendly, and one of the best ways to experience the city authentically is to strike up a chat with someone in a café or shop. You never know what hidden gems they might suggest. Whether it's a little-known restaurant, a secret garden, or an independent bookstore, the key is to engage with locals and let them guide you to the places they enjoy.

- Ask at your local café or pub about their favorite spots to eat, drink, or hang out, and you'll be surprised at the treasures you'll discover.

## CONCLUSION

London is a city that continually evolves, blending tradition with modernity in ways that captivate and inspire. As you step into the heart of this dynamic metropolis in 2025, you'll find a destination that offers not only iconic landmarks but also countless opportunities to explore, discover, and immerse yourself in its rich culture. Whether you're drawn to its history, arts, neighborhoods, or vibrant food scene, London has something for every traveler.

This guide has provided the insights, tips, and recommendations needed to make your visit meaningful and memorable. From the renowned attractions to hidden gems off the beaten path, you now have the tools to craft a journey that aligns with your interests, schedule, and budget.

Embrace the unexpected—whether it's stumbling upon a local market, enjoying a quiet moment in a lesser-known park, or finding inspiration in a hidden gallery. London's true beauty lies in its diversity and the personal experiences it offers. As you explore this remarkable city, remember that it's not just about ticking off a list of attractions, but about creating memories, forging connections, and making the city your own.

In 2025, London continues to be a city that invites exploration, adventure, and discovery. It's a place that rewards those who are curious, those who take the time to look beyond the surface, and those who approach it with an open mind and heart.

Your journey through London is just beginning, and the city has much to offer. The vibrant streets, cultural experiences, and moments of quiet wonder await you. Welcome to London—an unforgettable experience is just around the corner.

Printed in Great Britain
by Amazon